THE
PREDICTIVE
EDGE

THE
PREDICTIVE
EDGE

ALEJANDRO LOPEZ-LIRA

THE

PREDICTIVE

EDGE

OUTSMART THE MARKET

USING **GENERATIVE AI** AND **CHATGPT** IN

FINANCIAL FORECASTING

WILEY

Published by John Wiley & Sons, Inc., Hoboken, New Jersey.
Published simultaneously in Canada.

For general information on our other products and services or for technical support, please contact our Customer Care Department within the United States at (800) 762-2974, outside the United States at (317) 572-3993 or fax (317) 572-4002.

Wiley also publishes its books in a variety of electronic formats. Some content that appears in print may not be available in electronic formats. For more information about Wiley products, visit our website at www.wiley.com.

Library of Congress Cataloging-in-Publication Data is Available:

ISBN 9781394242719 (Cloth)
ISBN 9781394242726 (ePub)
ISBN 9781394242733 (ePDF)

Cover Design: Wiley
Cover Image: © iamchamp/Adobe Stock
Author Photo: Courtesy of the Author

SKY10075361_051724

To my wonderful wife Emma and my family.

Contents

Preface

What if artificial intelligence could accurately predict which stocks are about to increase in value? As an investor, you could know which companies to invest in before prices take off. This book explains how to use the most advanced artificial intelligence—ChatGPT—to invest better. It provides a step-by-step tutorial to forecast stock price movements and design and implement investment strategies using ChatGPT.

ChatGPT is the most sophisticated technology I have encountered. I was surprised by the immense capacity and sometimes cleverness that ChatGPT displays and how it vastly increased my productivity. For example, it made it trivial to proofread text, write code, brainstorm, and prototype sophisticated mathematical models. It has near (and sometimes better than) human-level skills in multiple domains, including writing, coding, and image generation. Could it also be used for investment prediction?

Stock market prediction methods have always intrigued me. I have researched (and occasionally deployed) them during my Ph.D. at Wharton and now at the University of Florida. ChatGPT's potential captivated me, and I was eager to solve related research questions. The first question was, can ChatGPT forecast stock price movements?

This book is based on an academic paper I wrote with Yuehua Tang in April 2023 to answer this question. We wanted to know if ChatGPT could accurately predict stock price movements using news headlines. The results were startling: ChatGPT was able to forecast positive returns with unparalleled precision. We simulated the returns of a strategy that followed ChatGPT's predictions on news data and found it would have produced more than 400 percent in just 18 months—compared to average annual stock market returns of around 10 percent.

The paper immediately grabbed media attention. I was interviewed live by CNN and other media outlets. Hundreds of online articles were written about it, and the research was downloaded more than 60,000 times (by far my most downloaded).

Research articles are dense and challenging to read because we want to be rigorous and consider all possibilities. We use obscure terminology that is familiar to academics but is hard to understand for everyone else not involved in the research. Yet, I receive constant emails about the research methodology and specifics of the article. There is broad interest in how ChatGPT can transform finance, but there are better ways to present the information than academic writing.

I drafted this book to make the research accessible and to reach a wider audience. *The Predictive Edge* is designed to contain practical but comprehensive information on using these new powerful technologies best. It is meant for people with little background in artificial intelligence or finance. You are not expected to be an expert, and I did my best to make my book as self-contained as possible, although you may want to search online or ask ChatGPT to clarify and exemplify some concepts.

Introduction

What if artificial intelligence could predict the stock market? Artificial intelligence (AI) is transforming numerous industries, and finance is no exception. Recent advances have led to sophisticated chatbots like ChatGPT with remarkable skills. The potential is enormous—if AI could predict price movements, investors would have an incredible advantage. However, while AI shows promise for finance, reliably forecasting complex financial markets is an immense challenge. *The Predictive Edge* examines the intriguing academic research documenting how ChatGPT can forecast stock price movements. It explains how to translate this theoretical knowledge into practical investment strategies, exploring how ChatGPT can be leveraged to predict stock prices accurately.

This book is grounded in academic research investigating a method using ChatGPT to predict whether news headlines indicate positive or negative returns for a stock. It presents the method and results in detail and provides a step-by-step guide to implementing the strategy, discussing practical considerations and refinements. We will follow the research and explore the promises and limitations of using natural language processing for finance.

The study's results are surprising. The strategy delivered more than 400% simulated returns in less than two years by going long on stocks with positive headlines and shorting negative headlines. In contrast, the stock market average is around 10% annually. While the research documents how ChatGPT captures valuable signals amid the endless news stream, *The Predictive Edge* aims to make these insights accessible to a broad audience with little background in AI.

Understanding these methods is increasingly relevant as the capability to quickly analyze vast volumes of text data represents a significant shift in stock trading. Traditional financial estimations often rely on charts, numbers, and fundamental analyses. These tools have served us well, but they are now being supplemented—and sometimes replaced—by algorithms and artificial intelligence.

Yet, the potential of AI in finance goes beyond simple speed. AI models can scan massive datasets for patterns that humans cannot see. They can also analyze many information sources simultaneously, from news articles and social media sentiment to economic indicators and earnings reports. This book thoroughly explains how to combine these technologies to produce valuable investment insights. It also explains the emerging landscape of finance and AI, providing valuable insights and strategies for investors, finance professionals, technologists, and anyone else interested in the convergence of these two fields.

What You Will Learn

The Predictive Edge will teach you how to exploit large language models' remarkable ability to process and analyze text-based data, such as news headlines, to predict potential effects on stock prices. We will learn about AI's influence on stock market trading and financial forecasting, emphasizing how AI and machine learning can be applied to make better investment decisions.

We will cover not only the theoretical concepts but also practical advice on how to incorporate advanced AI models into quantitative trading strategies. Whether you are an experienced investor, finance professional, business leader, or simply eager to apply AI in investment decisions, the material is relevant across multiple backgrounds. You will understand how to use these emerging technologies in investing or advancing your career.

Moreover, we will explore the advantages of AI-powered stock market forecasting and investment decision-making and address critical challenges in the modern investment landscape. We will examine how traditional stock market analysis methods can often overlook subtle market sentiments, leading to inaccuracies and potential financial losses.

We will study methods to overcome current limitations by building strong fundamentals of AI in financial forecasting and following practical guidance on integrating AI tools into investment decisions. By adequately leveraging AI's predictive strengths, you can work on achieving higher returns while constructing sturdier, more adaptive portfolios.

These technologies are evolving rapidly and understanding their current state is insufficient. Therefore, in addition to learning extensively about the existing tools, you will acquire a general framework to understand future advances in AI. The chapters will assist you in gaining a critical, forward-thinking perspective, enabling you to recognize the latest trends and developments.

Working through step-by-step frameworks and learning about the fundamental concepts will be valuable, especially if you are just acquiring a technical background but recognize the significance of AI in shaping the future of investing. The material will enable you to deploy AI for your financial and investment objectives.

After reading this book, you will:

♦ Understand core concepts of stock markets, AI, and natural language processing, and how they intersect
♦ Comprehend ChatGPT capabilities and limitations in depth, including ethical considerations
♦ Grasp the methodology and startling results of the ChatGPT forecasting study
♦ Have clear guidance for deploying similar trading strategies in the real world
♦ Appreciate versatile applications of language AI across financial workflows
♦ Recognize future opportunities and persistent challenges as AI transforms finance
♦ Feel equipped to apply these emerging technologies in your business or investments
♦ Be inspired by AI's potential while critically assessing its limitations
♦ Know the best practices to implement AI analytics responsibly and avoid pitfalls
♦ Remain updated on the state of the art in this rapidly evolving field

Applying AI in finance can be challenging, and a structured approach is critical to understanding AI's full potential. *The Predictive Edge* is your guide, providing a well-organized overview of AI in finance, from its fundamentals to advanced applications. Each chapter explains AI's workings, applications, and transformative potential in financial forecasting. If you follow the material, you will be prepared to understand the AI revolution in finance and gain the practical skills to succeed in this quickly developing field.

How This Book Is Structured

The Predictive Edge has three parts. Part I covers the fundamentals of finance and AI. Part II explores ChatGPT and its incorporation into investment strategies. Part III provides further applications and speculates about the future of AI and finance. Expert readers may want to skip Part I and return for reference, as necessary. We now briefly explore each chapter's contents.

Part I: Fundamentals

These first four chapters provide the essential baseline knowledge on stock markets, artificial intelligence concepts, natural language models, and ChatGPT required to comprehend the financial forecasting application covered later. By grounding core ideas from trading approaches to AI innovations, Part I aims to make the specifics of leveraging ChatGPT for stock predictions accessible even if you do not have a technical background in these areas.

CHAPTER 1: UNDERSTANDING THE STOCK MARKET

This chapter provides the fundamental background on stock markets, setting the foundation to understand how AI and ChatGPT could be applied for financial forecasting.

The chapter begins by covering market basics—economic functions, diverse types of markets such as derivatives, and significant investment instruments. We then explore key concepts around trading stocks—what they are, major participants, and standard analysis methods like fundamental, technical, and news/sentiment-driven approaches. We will also learn about portfolio management fundamentals and major investing strategies and how portfolio construction and risk management are instrumental in achieving investing success.

After covering the building blocks, the chapter explores current applications of AI in finance and stock prediction, providing context on the potential benefits and limitations of algorithmic forecasting. It concludes with a preview of core concepts covered in the next chapter and includes a check-your-understanding section and a recap to emphasize critical takeaways. These sections will also be present in all the following chapters.

Chapter 1 provides the necessary foundation for employing AI in forecasting by introducing key concepts—stocks, trading approaches, portfolios, and current applications of AI. The chapter contains the knowledge needed to help you understand the rest of the book, even if you are just getting familiar with the basics of investment and AI. The goal is to prepare you so the methods and results around forecasting are intuitive and meaningful when presented later.

CHAPTER 2: UNDERSTANDING ARTIFICIAL INTELLIGENCE

This chapter provides a high-level explanation of AI to comprehend core concepts behind technologies like ChatGPT. It starts by defining intelligence and discussing diverse aspects of human cognition that inspired the development of thinking machines.

We will then explore the history of efforts to create intelligent computers. We will study central innovations like machine learning and deep learning that enabled recent AI breakthroughs in accessible language, focusing on high-level intuitions rather than mathematical details.

Specifically, we will contrast the symbolic logic-based approach that initially dominated AI research against the data-driven machine learning paradigm that has recently gained prominence. We will also learn about the massive datasets and computational power needed to train deep neural networks behind state-of-the-art AI systems.

The chapter concludes by previewing how large language models represent the latest advancement in natural language processing, setting the stage for understanding ChatGPT's abilities for financial forecasting. The goal is to provide you with enough background without getting overly technical so ChatGPT's financial forecasting approach is intuitive when covered later.

CHAPTER 3: LARGE LANGUAGE MODELS: A GAME CHANGER

This chapter dives deeper into the AI concepts directly relevant to comprehending ChatGPT's abilities. We begin by exploring natural language processing (NLP)—the subdomain of AI focused on understanding, generating, and interacting with human languages. It also covers Core NLP tasks, algorithms, and applications.

We then explore generative AI, the technology behind content-creating systems like DALL-E for images and ChatGPT for text. We cover key capabilities like capturing patterns from vast datasets and using that learning to produce novel, high-quality outputs. Next, we will learn about the game-changing innovation of large language models (LLMs). LLMs like GPT-3 and Claude are foundationally transforming NLP by leveraging immense datasets and model sizes. We will cover their multivariate benefits over previous NLP systems and current limitations.

The goal is to provide an intuitive explanation of how advanced natural language systems work in order to understand the financial forecasting approach presented afterward.

CHAPTER 4: ADVANCED TOPICS IN LLMs

While the previous chapter overviews large language models, this chapter explores the fundamental architectures and mechanisms powering them. It starts by explaining technical elements like the self-attention layers and Transformer models that enabled exponential progress in language AI. We cover the intuitions behind these innovations without requiring a mathematical background. We then learn about the processes to improve LLMs, including Transfer learning to train on vast datasets and fine-tune them for specialized tasks. These techniques enabled models like ChatGPT to reach new performance heights. Finally, the chapter summarizes the landscape of significant LLMs, highlighting how capabilities proliferate.

Part II: ChatGPT and Stock Prediction

With foundational knowledge established in Part I, we now transition to Part II's comprehensive coverage of the chatbot stock prediction methodology, results, and practical implementation guidance. Chapters 5 through 8 contain the core content, spanning ChatGPT capabilities to groundbreaking findings and a step-by-step guide for deploying the strategies.

CHAPTER 5: WHAT IS ChatGPT?

This chapter comprehensively covers ChatGPT's capabilities, limitations, and best practices to apply the model effectively. It begins by discussing ChatGPT's diverse skills, like conversing naturally, following instructions, running code, browsing websites, understanding language, adapting to context, displaying world knowledge, generating creative content, adjusting in real time, and more. We also learn about safety and ethical considerations.

The chapter then outlines the current weaknesses of ChatGPT and similar LLMs such as lacking deeper understanding, short-term memory, sensitivity to input phrasing, potential hallucinations, and more. It also addresses ethical pitfalls and provides guidance on prompt engineering, covering best practices for structuring effective prompts to yield optimal chatbot performance. Templates and examples are included to help you craft high-quality prompts. Finally, the chapter covers business-use cases and ethical considerations around responsible deployment to encourage users to apply ChatGPT safely, accountably, and for social good.

The goal is to provide a comprehensive yet accessible guide so that users can maximize value from ChatGPT while proactively addressing risks and limitations.

CHAPTER 6: CAN CʜᴀᴛGPT FORECAST STOCK PRICE MOVEMENTS?

This chapter presents the core research on leveraging ChatGPT for stock prediction. It explains the empirical study methodology and results in detail. This chapter presents the book's academic foundation: the groundbreaking empirical evidence demonstrating ChatGPT's ability to forecast prices. The results' interpretation, evaluation, and discussion provide a research-backed perspective on the transformational potential of leveraging language AI in financial analysis while acknowledging current limitations and ethical considerations.

The methodology section covers the data collection, including integrating daily stock returns, news headlines, and relevance scores to filter noise, and carefully addressing look-ahead bias. It then presents the natural language prompt posed to ChatGPT to forecast returns. Next, the startling results are examined—more than 400% simulated profits in less than a year and a half. The chapter analyzes the findings and discusses implications for financial analysts, active trading strategies, the labor market, retail investors, regulations, and the long-term outlook for AI in finance.

CHAPTER 7: IMPLEMENTING A ChatGPT TRADING STRATEGY: A STEP-BY-STEP GUIDE

This chapter provides a thorough, step-by-step guide to implementing the ChatGPT-based stock forecasting approach for investment returns. It begins by presenting the overall market-neutral strategy framework. The chapter then addresses preliminary steps, such as setting goals, resource requirements, stock selection criteria, and risk management considerations.

The key processes of developing, backtesting, implementing, and monitoring the strategy are covered next in detail. The chapter discusses methods for position sizing, benchmarking, leveraging tools for automation, evaluating performance, and dynamically adjusting the model over time. It also explores compliance considerations.

The intention is to provide you with all the information you need to implement the ChatGPT trading methods. While results may vary in practice, this blueprint is designed to help investors succeed by providing the best practices refined through multiple rounds of research. The chapter serves as a bridge between abstract academic findings and practical application.

CHAPTER 8: ChatGPT IN ACTION: PRACTICAL APPLICATIONS

While the previous chapter focused on ChatGPT's stock forecasting strategy, this chapter explores integrating ChatGPT into broader financial contexts. It provides examples of combining natural language predictions with quantitative models for enhanced performance. Risk management use cases are then presented, leveraging ChatGPT to detect market regime changes and mitigate losses.

The chapter also discusses integration with automated trading systems for seamless implementation. Overall, it aims to spark ideas on versatile applications of ChatGPT in finance beyond stock prediction, including enhancing processes from data analysis to trade execution. The goal is to demonstrate the flexibility of AI to drive value across financial workflows—from research to risk management, reporting, and more.

Part III: Envisioning a Financial Future with AI

In the concluding section, the focus shifts from the details of forecasting methods to a broader perspective. We explore the future development of

AI in finance, including ongoing progress but also persistent difficulties related to trust and transparency. Part III concludes with final recommendations for innovating as algorithms transform investing.

CHAPTER 9: THE FUTURE OF AI IN FINANCIAL FORECASTING

This chapter explores the outlook and opens questions about the potentially transformational applications of AI in finance. It discusses continued progress in algorithms and models, with innovations in generative AI, reinforcement learning, Transfer learning, multimodal architectures, and more that are applicable to financial analysis. It also examines potential synergies with emerging technologies like blockchain and the internet of things.

The chapter then covers crucial areas like data quality and availability in improving predictions, personalization for individual investors, ethical risk mitigation, education to encourage responsible use, and understanding current AI limitations. Regulatory implications are also discussed as algorithms influence markets more.

Overall, this chapter aims to provide an insightful perspective on the future landscape for financial AI models based on the latest research—conveying promising opportunities but also addressing substantial challenges and open questions that persist.

CHAPTER 10: HOW AI IS SHAPING OUR ECONOMIC FUTURE

The concluding chapter recaps the core concepts covered and reflects on the significance of the chatbot stock prediction findings. It discusses practical implications, applications in finance, and best practices for responsibly integrating AI analytics.

It explores emerging trends in financial AI, forecasting the technology's future role in transforming areas from research to risk management. In addition, it addresses challenges and ethical considerations around bias, transparency, and misuse. It provides guidance for practitioners to stay atop rapid advancements, followed by a call to action for continuous innovation and community engagement as AI proliferates in finance. Finally, the chapter presents inspirational commentary on AI's transformative potential while also emphasizing the importance of human judgment in investment decision-making into the future.

The conclusion aims to provide a perspective on the immense promise and limitations of applying AI in finance, inspiring you to engage actively with these emerging capabilities.

PART I

Fundamentals

CHAPTER 1

Understanding the Stock Market

The stock market is crucial in modern financial markets. It helps generate wealth, reflects economic health, and drives growth. Companies use it to raise capital for expansion and innovation. Savers and investors participate in the market to grow their wealth, and it also serves as a direct expression of various economic indicators.

Stock markets, which have existed since the 1600s, started as physical locations where traders would meet to buy and sell shares but stock markets have since transitioned into digital platforms that operate worldwide. In the stock market, buyers and sellers trade stocks, representing ownership in public companies. These transactions involve much more than a simple money exchange for ownership rights. They combine economic indicators, investor sentiment, and global events. A high valuation of a company's stock often shows a vote of confidence from the markets. Conversely, declining stock prices can signify concerns about a company's prospects or broader economic issues.

The stock market impacts retirement portfolios, college savings plans, and even the economic policies of governments. Its movements can influence consumer and business confidence and shape spending and investment decisions on a global scale. Therefore, understanding the stock market goes beyond comprehending the rise and fall of individual stocks. It involves grasping the relationship between these movements and broader economic narratives and recognizing their impact.

This chapter will teach you about the stock market's core concepts. If you understand the stock market basics, learning the specifics of implementing trading strategies in future chapters will be easier. If you already possess extensive stock market knowledge, feel free to skim this chapter. However, if you are new to investing, reading and comprehending each concept is valuable.

We will start by briefly exploring the stock market's function and history. Next, we will examine different financial markets, each with a distinct role in the global financial ecosystem and some investment vehicles. You will then learn core concepts in stock trading, from what stocks (also called shares) are to the diverse market participants and their roles. This section will help you comprehend how stock markets function daily.

Analyzing stocks is historically more of an art than a science, and we will study the details and limitations of fundamental and technical analysis, two popular methodologies investors apply to select investment opportunities. Understanding how these approaches work is essential to engaging in the stock market because many participants use them, even if they have drawbacks.

Afterward, we will learn about portfolio management and trading strategies and discuss how to build and manage a diversified investment portfolio. Moreover, we will overview various investment approaches, from passive investment to value and growth investing.

By the end of this chapter, you will have a solid foundation in stock market basics. A solid understanding of these principles is necessary for using artificial intelligence (AI) in financial forecasting. As technologies like AI become more integrated with financial decision-making, having such knowledge becomes indispensable.

Stock Market Fundamentals

Investors actively buy and sell company shares in the stock market. The marketplace not only facilitates stock trading but also serves as a platform for companies to raise capital from the public. This capital is critical for companies to fund operations, innovate, and expand, thus making it vital to economic growth and development.

The stock market's significance extends beyond the corporate sphere. For investors, it represents a means to grow wealth and save to achieve long-term goals like retirement or education. For the economy, it acts as an indicator of health and confidence. Robust and active stock markets often signal a thriving economy, while downturns can show economic challenges. Policymakers, economists, and investors monitor the stock market's health, as it can offer significant insights into the economy.

HOW STOCK MARKETS CONTRIBUTE TO ECONOMIES

Stock markets fulfill several vital economic functions. First, they provide a mechanism for price discovery, where supply and demand meet to price publicly traded companies. This pricing mechanism is important as it reflects the market's collective judgment of a company's worth, based on its current performance and prospects.

Second, stock markets offer liquidity, allowing investors to buy or sell shares cheaply. This liquidity makes investing in stocks attractive and enables companies to raise capital more efficiently. When a company issues shares, it can tap into a broad pool of potential investors, often more helpful than seeking funding through loans.

Third, stock markets facilitate capital allocation. Efficient markets ensure that investment toward companies and industries performing well uses funds in the most productive way possible and has growth potential. This allocation plays a significant role in driving economic innovation and growth.

Finally, stock markets serve as a key barometer for the economy, reflecting investor sentiment and expectations about the future. Movements in stock prices can provide insights into how investors view the economy's health, influencing consumer confidence and business decisions.

The stock market's role in price discovery, providing liquidity, allocating capital, and serving as an economic indicator underscores its importance to investors, companies, and the broader economy. In addition to the stock market, other related financial markets support the financial ecosystem.

DIFFERENT FINANCIAL MARKETS

The financial market is a broad term encompassing various marketplaces where participants can trade financial assets, commodities, and other fungible value items at prices determined by supply and demand.

While the stock market is the most recognized form of a financial market, others exist, and understanding them is important.

These markets, which vary in scale, function, and the types of assets traded, collectively facilitate the efficient movement of capital and risk throughout the economy. They serve as venues for raising money, investing, risk management, and price discovery. Each market type has unique characteristics, rules, and participant dynamics, and each of these markets plays a specific role in the financial system:

◆ Stock Markets: They deal with trading shares, which are ownership units of companies. These markets are pivotal for companies seeking to raise capital and investors looking to buy partial ownership of these companies. Investors and policymakers often see stock markets as indicators of economic health and business prosperity.

◆ Bond Markets: Unlike stock markets, bond markets trade debt securities. This market allows governments, municipalities, and corporations to raise funds for various projects or operations. Investors (lenders) in bond markets provide money to the bond issuer (the borrower). In return, investors receive interest payments over time, plus the bond's total value when it comes due. Bond markets serve as interest rate and credit risk indicators.

◆ Commodities Markets: These markets involve trading physical goods or primary products such as gold, oil, and agricultural products. Commodities markets are vital for managing supply and demand dynamics across different industries, allowing producers and consumers to hedge against price volatility.

◆ Forex (Foreign Exchange) Markets: Investors trade currencies in the forex markets 24 hours a day, making it one of the most liquid markets. Forex markets are essential for global trade and finance integration, as they allow for exchanging different currencies, facilitating international business and investment.

Other complex financial instruments, like futures and options, are traded in derivatives markets. These instruments derive their value from the value of an underlying asset. The underlying assets usually include stocks, bonds, commodities, or currencies.

Futures are contracts allowing the buying or selling of an asset in the future at an agreed price. Exchanges standardize futures contracts in quantity and quality to simplify their trading. Investors employ futures for risk management or speculation. Options are instruments that give the holder the right to buy or sell an asset at a prespecified price before a specific date. But unlike futures, they do not require buying or selling the asset. Call options give the right to buy, and put options give the right to sell.

Participants can use derivatives as powerful tools for managing financial risk and speculative purposes. However, they can also be complex and carry high risk. Hence, it is imperative to comprehend these derivative instruments before trading them.

The financial market landscape is diverse, with each market type serving distinct purposes within the global economy. From providing avenues for raising capital (stock and bond markets) to facilitating international trade (forex market) and offering platforms for hedging against price volatility (commodities and derivatives markets), these markets are integral to the financial system. In Part II of the book, you will learn how these diverse markets present challenges and opportunities for AI-driven analysis and decision-making.

INVESTMENT VEHICLES IN THE STOCK MARKET

Before learning about the fundamental stock trading concepts, we must understand how investors can participate in the stock market. Different investment vehicles offer diverse levels of risk, management styles, and investment strategies.

- ◆ **Mutual Funds:** They gather money from many investors to create a managed portfolio of diverse stocks, bonds, or other securities. Investors buy shares in the fund to benefit from diversification and professional expertise. The fund regularly divides the total resources among various investments, like stocks or bonds. These instruments are ideal for those looking for diversified portfolios and professional management.
- ◆ **Exchange-Traded Funds (ETFs):** These instruments are investment funds traded on stock exchanges. ETFs track market indexes, commodities, or bundles of assets. They offer seamless flexibility, allowing investors to exchange them at market prices and low costs throughout the day.

- **Self-Managed Accounts:** For those who prefer a hands-on approach, self-managed accounts allow individuals to buy and sell stocks, bonds, and other securities according to their research and strategies. This method requires more knowledge and time investment but offers complete control over the trading decisions.
- **Robo-Advisors:** These automated platforms effortlessly create and manage a diversified portfolio. They use algorithms to select investments based on your risk tolerance and goals, making them an option for those seeking hands-off investment management.
- **Hedge Funds:** These are alternative investment funds that can pursue more complex trading strategies, like using leverage, trading derivatives, and short selling. Hedge funds typically require a high net worth to invest in them, but theoretically they can provide returns independent of overall market conditions.

Active managers of some mutual and hedge funds and investors with self-managed accounts typically engage in active stock trading.

Stock Trading

Stock trading is buying or selling company shares to generate a profit. It combines economic insights, market analysis, and a psychological understanding of the markets. While trading stocks might seem straightforward, the process involves understanding several fundamental principles. These principles include the mechanics of trading, the stocks available, the roles of various market participants, and the strategies deployed in trading decisions.

WHAT ARE STOCKS?

Stocks represent part ownership in a company. The term "share" is often used interchangeably with stocks, although it usually represents the units of stocks of a specific company. Individuals who buy a company's stock become shareholders. Investors own a fraction of a company in proportion to the total shares they purchase. For example, if a company has 100 million shares and you buy 1 million, you own 1% of the company.

Stocks can be common or preferred.

- Common Stocks: They are the most usual type of stock. They give shareholders voting rights, usually one vote per share owned. Shareholders sometimes receive dividends and can vote to choose company board members who oversee management decisions. Stock markets typically trade common stocks.
- Preferred Stocks: They rarely have voting rights but have a higher claim to company assets and earnings than common stocks. Preferred shareholders get dividend payments before common shareholders. In the event of company liquidation, they also receive payment before others.

Investors sometimes categorize companies by their market capitalization, which is the total market value of their outstanding shares. This classification helps investors understand the company's size and includes categories like large-cap, mid-cap, and small-cap. Small-cap shares have higher trading costs. Because of these high trading costs, many active portfolio managers avoid trading them. Since fewer market participants actively incorporate the latest information in them by trading, their returns are usually easier to predict. Because of their predictability, they are an excellent choice for investors, with low fees and minimal market impact.

MARKET PARTICIPANTS

The stock market has various participants, each playing a unique role. One of the key groups is individual investors, also called retail investors. These are everyday people who buy and sell stocks. They have distinct objectives, from building a portfolio for long-term goals like retirement or education savings to actively trading, hoping to achieve short-term gains.

Another significant group is institutional investors. This category includes pension funds, mutual funds, hedge funds, and insurance companies that invest sizeable sums of money. They can substantially influence market prices because of the size of their trades.

Brokers and dealers also play an important part. Brokers facilitate the buying and selling of stocks for clients, while dealers trade stocks for their accounts. Moreover, market makers provide liquidity by buying and selling stocks to ensure organized trading.

Lastly, regulators and central banks form an essential component of the market. Institutions such as the Securities and Exchange Commission (SEC) oversee the markets. Their primary goal is to guarantee fairness in trading and to uphold transparency in all market activities. Central banks control interest rates and affect firms' valuations. Sometimes, during extreme market periods, they also buy and sell instruments directly.

BUYING AND SELLING STOCKS

Besides the theoretical discussion, understanding the practical steps in buying and selling stocks is beneficial. Here are some potential specific steps.

1. **Opening a brokerage account:** To trade, an individual must open an account with a brokerage firm. This process involves providing personal information and answering questions about investment experience and risk tolerance.
2. **Researching:** Before investing, it is vital to study the stocks, which involves analyzing the company's financial statements, market position, and growth potential.
3. **Placing trades:** Traders can place orders to buy or sell stocks through a broker or an online trading platform. Common order types include market orders, limit orders, and stop-loss orders.

Market orders are instructions on buying or selling a financial instrument immediately at the current price. These orders ensure that the trade happens rapidly but do not guarantee the price. Second, limit orders instruct brokers to trade only at a specified price or better. Buy limit orders set the highest price to pay. Sell limit orders specify the lowest price to accept. Limit orders guarantee a price level, but not that the trade will happen.

Stop-loss orders are a more advanced type. A market stop-loss order attempts to limit an investor's loss in a trading position. Stop-loss orders set a trigger price to cut losses if a stock's price changes adversely. If the stock hits the trigger price, the order is executed as a market order at the next available price. Once the stock hits this price, the stop-loss order automatically converts into a market order and trades at the next available price. Stop-losses cap downside risk but do not guarantee the final sell price. In fast markets, the actual price can be much lower. Traders can place stop-loss orders for buying or selling.

Trading stocks involves regularly monitoring stock performance and staying informed about market conditions. Later in the chapter, we will learn how diversification, investing across various stocks or asset classes, can help you reduce risk. Now that you have learned about these foundational concepts, from understanding what stocks are to recognizing the roles of different market participants, we will look at classic investment strategies.

CLASSIC STOCK-PICKING STRATEGIES

Stock investment strategies involve identifying which companies to invest in. The analysis is not just about picking winners and avoiding losers; it is also a systematic approach to understanding a stock's potential risks and rewards. In this section, you will learn about two historical methods of stock research: fundamental analysis and technical analysis. Moreover, we will also cover news trading.

FUNDAMENTAL ANALYSIS

Fundamental analysis tries to calculate a stock's intrinsic value by studying how economic, financial, and other factors affect the company's value through its business and prospects. Investors perform several types of analysis with the hope of obtaining a measure of the "true" value of a stock:

- ◆ **Economic Analysis:** It involves looking at the overall economic environment, including factors like interest rates, inflation, and economic growth, and how it can affect a company's performance.
- ◆ **Industry Analysis:** Analyzing the industry involves understanding how the market works, including competition, growth opportunities, and regulations. This analysis helps in identifying the best-performing companies within a sector.

◆ **Company Analysis:** This is a thorough analysis of a company's financial statements—income statement, balance sheet, and cash flow statement. Analysts look at revenue, profit margins, return on equity, and earnings per share to gauge the company's financial health.

◆ **Valuation Metrics:** These include the price-to-earnings (P/E) ratio, price-to-book (P/B) ratio, dividend yield, and others. They help determine whether a stock is undervalued or overvalued compared to its historical performance or sector averages.

The intuition of fundamental analysis is that sometimes the current market value of a company differs from its intrinsic or true value since investors may not always price every company correctly. This strategy tries to assess a company's fair value, but several limitations can complicate the process:

◆ **Intrinsic Value Subjectivity:** Fundamental analysis involves estimating the inherent value of a stock based on economic, financial, and industry data. However, this process is highly subjective. Due to varying assumptions and models, analysts may produce different valuations based on the same data.

◆ **Impact of Non-Quantifiable Factors:** Management quality, brand value, and market competition are challenging to quantify but they significantly affect a company's performance. Fundamental analysis that is based on firms' financials might not fully account for these qualitative aspects.

◆ **Delayed Reflection of Current Events:** Fundamental indicators, like earnings reports, economic data releases, and industry trends, are historical and may not reflect the latest market changes or future uncertainties. As a result, investors might react slowly to new developments.

◆ **Market Irrationality:** Sometimes, the market does not behave rationally, and stock prices do not reflect underlying fundamentals because of speculative activities, market sentiment, or other macroeconomic factors. While fundamental analysis hopes the prices will correct in the future, this correction may take too long, and investors may be forced to close their positions with losses.

- **Estimating Future Earnings:** While earnings per share (EPS) or price-to-earnings (P/E) ratios are staples in fundamental analysis, forecasting future earnings is uncertain. Various unpredictable factors, such as market disruptions, new competitors, regulatory changes, or global events, can influence a company's future profitability. Relying on projected earnings can sometimes lead investors astray when these projections are based on optimistic or pessimistic assumptions.

- **The Unreliability of Book Value:** The price-to-book (P/B) ratio is a fundamental analysis signal based on a company's book value. However, a company's assets minus its liabilities can sometimes mislead book value because it does not correctly quantify intangible assets such as brand value and intellectual property. Outdated asset valuations or unaccounted liabilities can skew the accurate picture. Relying on the P/B ratio can cause misjudgments about a company's intrinsic value.

Technical Analysis

Unlike fundamental analysis, technical analysis assumes that historical trading activity and price changes can be reliable indicators of future stock performance. Technical analysts use various graphical displays of price volume called price charts. These include line, bar, and candlestick charts. Each type of chart depicts unique insights into market behavior. Traders try to predict future prices by examining these charts using some standard techniques, including:

- **Trend Analysis:** They identify the market's direction or a specific stock's price. Trends can be upward, downward, or sideways and are crucial to technical analysis.

- **Technical Indicators and Patterns:** Analysts use a range of indicators with distinctive names like moving averages, Relative Strength Index (RSI), and Bollinger Bands. They also look for patterns like head and shoulders, double tops and bottoms, and others that historically show potential market moves.

- **Volume Analysis:** Examining trading volume can, in theory, show if a price trend is reliable. Higher volumes validate the trend, while lower volumes may suggest a lack of conviction among traders.

♦ **Sentiment Analysis:** It involves assessing the overall mood of the market, which can be bullish (expecting prices to rise) or bearish (expecting prices to fall). News events, market rumors, and investor psychology can influence sentiment.

Despite the academic skepticism about technical analysis, it remains a widely employed technique. One theory is that it works because of **self-fulfilling prophecies**. Suppose many traders believe in a particular technical signal (e.g., a moving average crossover) and act upon it. In that case, their collective actions can indeed influence the stock price in the expected direction. The price change can be unrelated to the inherent validity of the signal and, instead, happen because the signal triggers a herd behavior among the traders that follow it.

Like fundamental analysis, technical analysis also has several limitations:

♦ **Pattern Reliability:** Technical analysis assumes that history repeats. However, the reliability of patterns and trends is often questionable, as unexpected market events or news can disrupt them, leading to false signals.

♦ **Overemphasis on Price Data:** Technical analysis predominantly focuses on price movements and volume, potentially overlooking broader economic or sectoral trends affecting a stock's future performance.

♦ **Over-Reliance on Past Data:** Technical analysis is retrospective. It assumes that historical price movements can predict future performance. However, many unpredictable factors influence stock markets, from sudden geopolitical events to surprise earnings reports. Relying only on past patterns can often leave traders ill-prepared for unexpected market shifts.

Besides theoretical limitations, technical analysis techniques face practical challenges during implementation:

♦ **Overwhelming Number of Indicators:** There are hundreds of indicators in technical analysis, and their number can be overwhelming. The variety of tools may lead traders to become flooded with conflicting signals and struggle to make optimal trading decisions.

♦ **Subjectivity:** Two traders looking at the same chart will reach different conclusions. Subjectivity is likely to arise if the analysts have strong feelings about the firm being analyzed or feel happy or sad that day. It can lead to inconsistent predictions.

♦ **Lack of Fundamental Consideration:** Technical analysis, in its purest form, disregards a company's fundamentals. Price and volume trend data can provide insights into short-term market sentiment but do not reveal a company's underlying health or potential. Ignoring fundamentals can sometimes lead to missed opportunities or undue risks, especially in the long term.

♦ **Short-Term focus:** Many technical analysis strategies target short-term trading opportunities. This horizon can be advantageous for day traders or swing traders but may not align with investors' goals for long-term growth and value. Relying only on technical analysis can be impractical for those with extended investment horizons.

Further, several practical implementation challenges apply to fundamental and technical analysis:

♦ **Cost:** One of the primary drawbacks of these techniques is their cost-intensive nature. Fundamental analysis requires extensive time and money to review companies' finances, industry reports, and economic data. Technical analysis is expensive because of the need for continuous market monitoring and time investment in learning various tools. Hiring skilled analysts, purchasing detailed reports, and dedicating time to in-depth research can be very costly, especially for smaller firms with fewer resources.

♦ **Scalability:** These approaches are not scalable. As an investment firm expands its portfolio, the requisite research grows, creating a bottleneck effect. Studying many companies in various sectors and regions increases complexity and complicates maintaining accuracy and detail.

♦ **Undiversified Portfolios:** Given the intensive research process, investors relying only on fundamental or technical analysis might end with a concentrated portfolio. In-depth research can inadvertently cause overconfidence in a few stocks, raising the risk of sector or company-specific downturns. Such a strategy can lead to heightened portfolio volatility, especially if one or more of these "high conviction" stocks underperform.

♦ **Challenges for Non-Experts:** For retail investors or those without a background in finance, diving deep into financial statements or price charts can be intimidating. Understanding the details of financial signals and their future impact on stocks is challenging and requires much learning. Many investors lack the expertise, patience, or interest to understand financial statements or learn charting tools and indicators.

These high costs, scalability issues, and investor biases can lead to volatility and suboptimal returns. Subjective interpretations and inherent complexities limit the accuracy of predictions in market analysis. In contrast, news trading is a more straightforward trading strategy. In the later chapters, we provide a step-by-step guide to implementing a news trading strategy.

NEWS TRADING AND SENTIMENT ANALYSIS

News trading involves buying or selling stocks based on news announcements. Significant economic reports, earnings announcements, and geopolitical developments can lead to abrupt and sizable movements in stock prices. News trading often relies on sentiment analysis, which involves evaluating the tone and context of textual data to determine investors' collective attitude or sentiment toward a particular stock or the market overall. It uses multiple data sources, including news articles, social media posts, and financial reports. Investors approach sentiment analysis using two methods: manual and automatic.

Manual Sentiment Analysis

Manual sentiment analysis involves analysts reading, interpreting, and categorizing content (like news articles, tweets, or forum posts) to determine the sentiment toward a stock or the overall market.

Humans are naturally good at understanding context, sarcasm, and nuanced language that automated systems might miss. Still, this technique has its limitations. For example:

♦ **Scalability:** Classifying texts by hand is labor-intensive and time-consuming, making analyzing large volumes of data costly.

♦ **Subjectivity:** Different analysts might interpret the same information differently, leading to inconsistent results.

♦ **Slower Process:** The time to read and interpret can lead to delayed reactions in fast-moving markets.

Automatic Sentiment Analysis

Automatic sentiment analysis uses software to quantify news sentiment. It has the advantage of handling large amounts of data, and unlike humans, machines apply the same standards across all data, leading to consistent analysis. Yet, several limitations remain:

♦ **Contextual Misunderstanding:** News articles and reports often contain nuances, sarcasm, or context-dependent meanings that early sentiment analysis tools cannot detect.

♦ **Dependence on Quality Data:** The performance depends on the training data quality.

♦ **Complex Set-Up:** Requires expertise to set up and maintain models, and there is a need for continuous updates as language changes.

While the early automatic sentiment analysis tools have many limitations, recent advances in AI have produced models capable of dealing with these nuances. The book's later chapters explain how ChatGPT can ease some of these limitations. Lastly, both the manual and automatic approaches face practical implementation challenges:

♦ **Lack of Contextual Understanding:** Non-expert investors and simple algorithms may misunderstand the sentiment of a news article or announcement. For example, some investors may view a news report about a company cutting costs positively, which can increase profit margins in the short term.

However, if the cut is in research and development, and the market understands it will lead to decreased profits in the future, the news can lead to a price decline. Traditional sentiment analysis tools and non-expert investors may miss such subtle differences.

- **Overreliance:** Non-professional investors, eager to leverage sentiment analysis, often rely too heavily on these tools, treating them as definitive predictors. This overreliance can lead to overlooking other critical market indicators.

- **Misunderstanding Market Reactions:** Retail investors and classic algorithms without a deep understanding can misjudge how other investors, especially institutional ones, would react to certain news. Even if a sentiment analysis tool labeled news "positive," investors might perceive it differently.

- **Lack of Comprehensive Coverage:** The overload of news sources available means that non-expert retail investors might only focus on mainstream news. Without a systematic approach, they risk overlooking significant pieces of information.

- **Emotional Bias:** When combined with personal biases, sentiment analysis tools can amplify the potential for misguided choices. A retail investor holding a positive bias toward a particular stock might give more weight to positive sentiment analysis, overlooking other negative signals from different estimation methods and leading to confirmation bias.

- **Trading Speed:** Sentiment analysis tools and human investors may not be able to react as quickly as high-frequency algorithmic trading systems to news events. By the time an insight or trade signal is generated, algorithms may have already capitalized on the event, and prices may have shifted. This makes trading on sentiment challenging.

Fortunately, as we will cover in the following chapters, AI can complement traditional methods, offering more dynamic, comprehensive, and data-driven approaches to stock market analysis.

Portfolio Management and Trading Strategies

Understanding the basics of portfolio management and trading strategies is fundamental to investing in the stock market. While stock analysis helps investors decide which stocks to buy or sell, portfolio management and trading strategies determine how these decisions fit into a broader investment plan.

BASICS OF PORTFOLIO MANAGEMENT

Portfolio management involves creating and maintaining an investment portfolio that aligns with an investor's goals, risk tolerance, and investment horizon. Effective portfolio management and trading strategies are instrumental in achieving investment goals.

One of the core principles of portfolio management is diversification, which involves spreading investments across distinct assets or asset classes to mitigate risk. Diversification reduces a portfolio's volatility, as the better performance of some investments can offset the poor performance of others. Distributing across asset classes that do not move together is even better.

In asset allocation, investors weigh different categories of assets in a portfolio. These categories include stocks, bonds, and cash. The distribution should reflect the investor's risk tolerance, investment objectives, and time horizon. Regularly reviewing and rebalancing a portfolio is key to maintaining the desired asset allocation. This process involves buying or selling assets in the portfolio to match the original or updated investment strategy.

Classical investing approaches range from active trading to passive investing. Trading strategies like value investing, growth investing, and others offer suggestions for stock selection based on individual investment preferences and risk tolerance. In contrast, passive investing involves buying and holding a diversified portfolio for a lengthy period.

COMMON INVESTMENT APPROACHES

The most straightforward and most recommended strategy is passive investing. Passive investors invest long term, avoiding the frequent buying and selling of stocks. The most common form of passive investing involves buying index funds or ETFs that track a market index like the S&P 500. Passive investors aim to replicate market performance instead of trying to beat the market. By not trading frequently, passive investors save on transaction fees and incur lower management fees, primarily when invested in index funds or ETFs. Passive strategies often involve a diversified portfolio that mirrors a broad market index, spreading risk across various sectors and assets.

Value investing is an active strategy involving buying undervalued stocks at lower prices than their intrinsic value. Investors using this strategy believe the market overreacts to news, resulting in stock price movements that do not reflect a company's long-term fundamentals. The technique involves buying stocks at lower prices than their fair value and selling them once the price reflects their true worth. The non-trivial part involves correctly perceiving a company's future value and resisting price fluctuations until the hypothetical price convergence.

In contrast, growth investors seek companies exhibiting above-average growth. The focus is on companies expected to grow at a fast pace compared to others in the market. Often, these companies will appear overpriced with metrics like the price-to-earnings ratio. Investors expect their fundamental operations to increase and drive the stock price up. However, there is a risk that these optimistic expectations will not materialize.

Another popular strategy is income investing, which focuses on generating a steady income from investments. Investors look for securities that pay dividends or interest, including bonds, dividend-paying stocks, and real estate investment trusts (REITs).

Moreover, in contrarian investing, investors buy stocks when others are selling and sell when others are buying. They believe they can capitalize on significant market mispricings in securities caused by herd behavior. In contrast, momentum investment follows the markets and buys when everyone buys.

Investors convinced that the market overvalues a stock sometimes use short-selling strategies. Shorting or short selling comprises borrowing a stock, selling it, hoping the price will fall, repurchasing it later at a lower price, and paying back the interest. Investors put assets in collateral to borrow the stock. For example:

1. Suppose you think Stock Y's price of $100 is too high and consider the correct value is $80. You expect the market to understand that the price is too high at some point.
2. To capitalize on this overpricing, you borrow one share of stock.
   a. You must repay one share of stock Y plus interest.
3. You leave $100 of cash as collateral.
   a. You will get back your collateral when you repay the share.

4. You sell the share and receive $100 to invest elsewhere or hold.
5. The next day, you close the position.
  a. Because it is a very short horizon, we will round interest to zero. For longer horizons, it is important to consider the cost of interest.
6. If the price is below $100, you make money.
  a. You repurchase it for, say, $95.
  b. Pay it back for $105.
  c. In total, you make $110 − $95 − $10 = $5.
  d. Since you started with $100 of collateral (that you get back), you get a return of 5% = $5/$100.
7. Otherwise, you lose any difference above $100.

These strategies can have limited upside (since the price is at least zero) and unlimited downside (since the price can keep increasing). Hence, they require very sophisticated risk-management techniques.

Finally, there are some advanced strategies called long-shorts. Long-short strategies seek to profit from both rising and falling prices in the market. Long-shorts involve taking concurrent long positions (buying securities expected to increase in value) and short positions (short selling securities expected to decrease in value). These strategies require an initial amount of equity to leave as collateral. The goal is for the long positions to outperform the shorts, providing an overall net gain regardless of broader market direction.

A portfolio with zero cost combines matched long and short positions in correlated securities to eliminate market exposure and risk. By weighting the long and short positions, the portfolio ensures that their price movements counterbalance each other. This strategy leads to a portfolio with no net market exposure and no inherent risk based on broader market fluctuations. The goal is to capture profits from relative mispricings between the securities.

Having covered some basic investment approaches, we will now transition to how to evaluate whether a strategy is successful.

PORTFOLIO PERFORMANCE METRICS

Before delving into how to measure investment performance, we need to understand some definitions. This material is usually covered in the first part of a semester-long college course. Still, we will go over a summarized version:

- **Return (percentage):** The percentage profit of the investment over a period. Returns are equal to the final value, including dividends and interest minus the initial value as a percentage of the initial value. Return = (Final Value − Initial Value)/Initial Value. For example, if you buy a stock at $100, receive a dividend during the period of $5 (and do not reinvest it), and sell at $120, the return is ($120 + $5 − $100)/$100 = 25/100 = 25%.
- **Risk-free rate:** The rate of return of investing in a safe asset (that always pays the same amount). The rate at which the U.S.A. borrows money is used to calculate the risk-free rate.
- **Excess return:** The return minus the risk-free rate.
- **Beta:** It measures the systematic volatility of an investment or portfolio compared to the market. Investors calculate it by comparing the covariance of the investment's returns with the market's returns divided by the market variance.
  - Beta = Cov(return, market return)/Var(market return)
  - A beta greater than one implies that the investment has more extreme movements than the market in the same direction as the market.
- **The Capital Asset Pricing Model (CAPM)** is a theory that predicts that a stock's expected excess return equals its beta times the expected excess return of the market. E[excess return] = beta*E[market's excess return].
- **Alpha** is the difference between an investment's average excess returns and the CAPM prediction. A positive alpha means the investment has performed better than its beta would predict, and vice versa.
- **Volatility**, the return's standard deviation, measures riskiness.
- The **Sharpe ratio,** an investment's average excess returns divided by its standard deviation, quantifies the tradeoff between risk and reward.
- The **Sortino ratio** is the average excess returns divided by the semi-deviation. It serves as another measure of risk, focusing only on the downside volatility.

◆ **Maximum drawdown (MDD)** quantifies the largest percentage drop from the highest portfolio value (peak) to the lowest value (trough) before achieving a new height. It calculates the maximum loss an investor would have experienced during a specific time frame. For example, if the portfolio starts at $50, doubles to $100, falls to $80, and recovers to $110, the maximum drawdown is (100 − 80)/100 = 20%.

Investors typically assess portfolio performance by combining these metrics. Looking at the total performance captured by the returns and the risk-adjusted performance is crucial. The alpha generally measures this performance, which assesses how the investment performed after accounting for market risk. The volatility and the maximum drawdown ordinarily measure risk. You want high returns with high alpha and low risk. Performance metrics will become helpful in later chapters when we implement a strategy step by step.

While this chapter may seem a little abstract, comprehending the fundamentals of the stock market sets a robust foundation for understanding AI's transformative role in finance. ChatGPT is opening new investment opportunities, but it is imperative to learn the basics first to exploit them. The effectiveness of these new technologies is grounded in a deep understanding of stock market fundamentals.

Summary

In this chapter, we worked on understanding the fundamentals of the stock market. First, we explored the vital functions of the stock market in enabling trading, raising capital, allocating resources efficiently, and indicating economic health. You learned about related financial markets like bonds, commodities, forex, and derivatives, which also play critical economic roles. We covered how stocks represent ownership and how vehicles like mutual funds, ETFs, self-managed accounts, and robo-advisors allow market participation.

Next, we studied the fundamentals of trading, which involve buying and selling stocks through a broker for profit. You learned how stocks are classified by market capitalization and differ as common (with voting rights) or preferred (with higher dividends). We overviewed key market participants like investors, brokers, dealers, and regulators that enable organized trading. We also learned about the different types of orders, like limit, market, and stop-loss.

Then, we explored popular techniques like fundamental analysis to estimate intrinsic value and technical analysis to study price charts. We covered how both face limitations like subjectivity. We also learned about news trading, which leverages sentiment analysis of announcements, either manually or using algorithms, to make timely decisions.

After that, we dived into effective portfolio management and how to align investments to goals through diversification and asset allocation while balancing risk. You learned about common long-term strategies like passive investing, value, growth, and income investing. We also covered contrarian approaches like short-selling and long-shorts.

Finally, we studied some terms that help us understand portfolio performance: returns, alpha, beta, volatility, and Sharpe ratio. We explored how returns quantify profits, alpha measures excess returns, beta captures market risk, volatility calculates investment risk, and the Sharpe ratio evaluates risk-adjusted returns.

Coming Up Next

The upcoming chapter, "Understanding Artificial Intelligence," examines the heart of AI. It covers fundamental definitions and the mechanisms that allow machines to learn, adapt, and outperform human capabilities in specific tasks. We explore the progression from traditional machine learning to the more sophisticated deep learning, which underpins many of today's financial forecasting tools.

Check Your Understanding Questions

- ◆ Stock Market Basics:
  - What is the stock market's primary function, and how does it contribute to the economy?
  - Differentiate between common and preferred stocks. What are the key differences in terms of rights and benefits for shareholders?

- Financial Market Types:
  - Compare and contrast the following financial markets: stock, bond, commodities, and forex. What unique characteristic does each market possess?
  - Explain the concept of a derivatives market. How do derivatives like futures and options function?
- Trading Principles:
  - Describe the role of market makers in the stock market. Why are they essential for maintaining market liquidity?
  - What is a dividend, and how does it influence the investment appeal of a stock?
- Stock Analysis Techniques:
  - Fundamental vs. Technical Analysis: Outline the primary focus of each analysis method and give an example of how each is applied in stock trading.
  - Why is volume critical in technical analysis? What information does it provide to traders?
- Portfolio Management:
  - What is diversification in portfolio management, and why is it considered an essential strategy for risk management?
  - Describe the concept of asset allocation. How does it differ for investors with varying risk tolerances and investment horizons?
- Trading Strategies:
  - Define value investing and growth investing. What are the primary criteria used in each strategy to select stocks?
  - What is passive investing, and how does it differ from other trading strategies regarding goals and methods?

CHAPTER 2

Understanding Artificial Intelligence

Artificial intelligence often evokes images of humanoid robots, self-driving cars, and futuristic cities. While these are facets of AI's potential, its true power lies in its ability to process vast amounts of data, recognize patterns, and make predictions with an accuracy that often surpasses human capabilities. These capabilities are a vital component of modern investment strategies.

This chapter examines artificial intelligence, its history from machine learning to deep learning, and the importance of large language models in financial forecasting. AI is more than a tool or a technology; it is a paradigm shift, a new way of understanding finance. As we will explore in later chapters, AI is becoming an integral tool for processing market data, identifying trends, and even directly trading stocks with superhuman proficiency.

By first building a foundation for understanding key AI concepts in this chapter, you will be better equipped to see how artificial intelligence transforms investing. From using AI for sentiment analysis of market-moving news to creating agents capable of high-frequency trading, the connections between AI and stock market forecasting will become clear as we progress. For now, we start by understanding the basics of AI.

What Is Artificial Intelligence?

To understand artificial intelligence, we briefly need to explore what "intelligence" is. We first break the concept of intelligence into understanding and adaptability, and application and abstract thinking[1] (Merriam-Webster n.d.).

Understanding and Adaptability
Intelligence is deeply rooted in adaptability and learning. It is not just about accumulating knowledge but about how we interact with and navigate new or challenging scenarios, underscoring the ability to evolve, adapt, and overcome. When faced with unfamiliar situations, intelligent beings do not merely react; they analyze, learn, and devise strategies to handle the situation. This capacity to reason, entertain options, and make informed decisions has allowed humanity to thrive in diverse environments and circumstances throughout history.

In stock markets and investing, human intellect plays an equally vital role. The ability to continuously analyze new information and understand market shifts has long been essential for investors to prosper.

Application and Abstract Thinking
Beyond mere understanding, intelligence also encompasses the application of knowledge. It is one thing to know but another to apply that knowledge effectively to manipulate one's surroundings or achieve specific goals. This application is evident in everything from constructing architectural marvels to developing advanced technological tools.

Furthermore, the ability to think abstractly to conceptualize ideas beyond the tangible and immediate is a hallmark of advanced intelligence. This abstract thinking has led to philosophical inquiries, scientific theories, and artistic expressions. In the stock market, investors use their existing knowledge and abstract reasoning to analyze market trends, select optimal investments, and shape their portfolios.

Intelligence is a dynamic interplay of learning, reasoning, application, and abstract thinking; empowering individuals to understand and shape their world. This concept sets the stage for exploring the diverse cognitive abilities and multiple intelligences landscape.

Different Kinds of Human Intelligence
Traditionally, intelligence was often equated with logical reasoning or linguistic ability. However, modern understandings recognize a

---
[1] We adapt the concept from the standard dictionary definition: *INTELLIGENCE.*

broader range of cognitive capacities and talents. There are multiple types of intelligence, each valuable in its own right.

Howard Gardner, a renowned psychologist from Harvard University, developed the theory of multiple intelligences, suggesting that humans possess various distinct intelligences (Cherry 2023; Gardner 1993; Warrington 2023).

- Verbal intelligence: The ability to communicate effectively through spoken and written language.
- Logical-mathematical intelligence: deductive reasoning and problem-solving skills.
- Spatial intelligence refers to the skill of visualizing and manipulating physical objects in a spatial context.
- Musical intelligence: the capacity to recognize and produce musical tones, rhythms, and patterns.
- Bodily-kinesthetic intelligence: using one's body skillfully and handling objects adeptly.
- Interpersonal intelligence: involves understanding and interacting effectively with others.
- Intrapersonal intelligence: It is a deep self-understanding of one's emotions, motivations, and goals.
- Naturalistic intelligence involves identifying and classifying diverse natural world components, such as plants, animals, and other natural phenomena.

An intriguing question arises with the diverse forms of intelligence, from linguistic to naturalistic: How do we accurately measure these varied types of human intelligence?

How Do We Measure Human Intelligence?

The goal is to quantify cognitive abilities and potential, but the process is complex due to the diverse nature of intelligence itself. The Intelligence Quotient (IQ) test is the most used method for measuring cognitive abilities. Developed initially by Binet in France, its primary purpose was identifying school children needing additional academic support (Binet, Simon, and Kite 2017).

An IQ test assesses various cognitive abilities, including logical reasoning for problem-solving, mathematical skills for numerical analysis, linguistic skills for vocabulary and comprehension, spatial relations for visualizing shapes, and memory for information recall. The resulting score is normalized, with an average score typically set at 100. Scores above or below this average denote above-average or below-average IQ, respectively.

While traditional measures like the IQ test focus on evaluating logical, mathematical, linguistic, and spatial abilities, they may only capture a fraction of the broad spectrum of human intelligence that Gardner and others have identified. This selective assessment leads us to ponder the nature of intelligence more comprehensively: Can these varied components of intelligence be mirrored in computers? Are computers capable of exhibiting forms of intelligence akin to humans?

Understanding Computers and Their Components

Before analyzing their capabilities, we explore the essential components underlying computers and artificial intelligence systems. Understanding the elements of computers and artificial intelligence is crucial, as it allows us to grasp how they function and the boundaries of their capabilities. Once familiar with these components, we can explore higher-level measures of AI's abilities, deficits, and potential. Understanding these capabilities will help determine how AI can help us make investment decisions.

Computers and Hardware Computers are electronic devices capable of performing complex calculations and tasks. They comprise hardware, physical components like the central processing unit (CPU), memory, and storage devices. Hardware is the foundational structure that enables a computer to function, process data, and execute instructions. Computers and hardware provide the necessary infrastructure for operating software and AI models.

Software Software encompasses the various programs and operating systems that function on computers and other hardware devices. It contains everything from the operating system that oversees hardware resources to application software designed for specific activities such as word processing, web browsing, or gaming. Software is the intermediary between the user and the computer's hardware, translating user commands into actions executed by the hardware.

Algorithms Algorithms are rules or instructions designed to perform specific tasks or solve problems. In computing, algorithms are implemented through software. They form the logic behind computer programs, enabling software to process data, make decisions, and perform operations.

Robots Robots are machines designed to carry out complex actions automatically, often using a combination of hardware and software. They can range from industrial robots used in manufacturing to service robots in healthcare. Robots typically use sensors and actuators (hardware) controlled by software algorithms to interact with the physical world. Robots combine hardware and software to interact autonomously with their environment.

AI Models Artificial intelligence models or AI systems are advanced algorithms designed to mimic human cognitive functions like learning, reasoning, and problem-solving. AI models often use machine learning, a subset of AI, where models are trained on data to make predictions or decisions. These models require powerful hardware, like graphics processing units (GPUs) for complex computations and are implemented through sophisticated software.

We use computers and algorithms as synonyms for AI models when it is clear.

Computer Capabilities Modern computers have advanced to a point where they exhibit remarkable capabilities beyond basic computation and, sometimes, beyond what humans can do.

- ◆ Learning and adaptation: Contemporary computers, driven by machine learning algorithms, can assimilate information from data and modify their behavior accordingly. For instance, a neural network trained on image data can learn to recognize and categorize objects in images.
- ◆ Reasoning: Certain AI systems are designed to reason based on the provided data. IBM Watson demonstrates automated reasoning abilities by using natural language processing, hypothesis generation and evaluation, gathering of supporting evidence, probabilistic confidence scoring, and dynamic learning to

answer questions accurately across different domains. Watson defeated human champions on Jeopardy by comprehending clues, evaluating multiple answer options based on its knowledge base, and determining the highest-probability response using supporting evidence for each option.

♦ Problem-solving: Computers can be programmed or trained to solve intricate problems, from optimizing logistics for global supply chains to finding the shortest route in a navigation system.

♦ Processing speed: Computers can handle immense quantities of information at speeds beyond human comprehension, providing them a superior edge in tasks demanding quick data analysis.

Despite the capabilities of modern computers and AI, we should recognize their inherent limitations and the ethical considerations they prompt.

♦ Lack of consciousness: While computers can process data and make decisions based on algorithms, they lack consciousness, self-awareness, and emotions. Their "decisions" lack feelings, intuition, or moral judgment.

♦ Dependence on human-defined parameters: AI systems operate within the confines of their programming or the parameters of their training data. They do not possess innate curiosity or the ability to question beyond their defined scope.

♦ Absence of generalization: While there is ongoing research in developing general AI, most current AI systems are specialized for specific tasks. Unlike humans, who can learn and adapt to various situations, a computer trained for one job might be incompetent at another.

♦ Ethical concerns: The idea of computers making decisions, especially in critical areas like healthcare or law enforcement, raises ethical concerns. Without human-like moral reasoning, can we trust computers to make decisions aligned to societal values?

These capabilities and concerns reveal more profound philosophical questions about machine intelligence. As computers demonstrate advanced capabilities like reasoning and problem-solving, it prompts the timeless debate: Can machines be intelligent? Or is human cognition fundamentally unique? Answering these questions will help us understand the limitations of how AI can improve investment decisions.

CAN COMPUTERS BE INTELLIGENT?

Whether computers can be intelligent becomes an even more pertinent question as artificial intelligence (AI) and machine learning technologies advance unprecedentedly. When we talk about computer intelligence, we often refer to a machine's ability to perform tasks that, when done by humans, would require intelligence.

Computers equipped with advanced AI algorithms exhibit a form of intelligence, but it is fundamentally different from human intelligence. They excel in processing, pattern recognition, and data-driven decision-making but lack the consciousness, emotions, and moral reasoning inherent to humans.

While they might mimic certain intelligent behaviors, the underlying processes are based on data and algorithms, not genuine understanding or consciousness. It is crucial to approach the concept of computer intelligence with a nuanced perspective, recognizing its potential and inherent differences from human cognition.

As AI advances, striking this balance becomes increasingly important in the financial sector. Algorithms can analyze market data and react to shifts faster than human traders but may lack intuitive judgment. AI tools help investors leverage powerful processing abilities, but so far, they do not replicate human behaviors like greed and panic that often irrationally move markets. Nevertheless, if computers have a form of intelligence, how can we measure it?

Measuring the intelligence of AI: The Turing Test

In his seminal 1950 work "Computing Machinery and Intelligence," Alan Turing proposed the Turing Test as a pragmatic approach to assessing machine intelligence, focusing on whether a machine can exhibit human-like conversational abilities rather than delving into the philosophical question of "Can machines think?" (Turing 1950). The test involves an interrogator trying to distinguish between humans and machines based solely on their text-based responses.

If the machine's responses are indistinguishable from the human's, it is considered to have passed the test.

The Turing Test has been pivotal in AI by emphasizing human-like intelligence as a benchmark. It encouraged AI to evolve beyond basic computational tasks to complex language understanding and conversation, fostering advancements in natural language processing (NLP) and machine learning (ML). This focus has led to AI systems capable of more nuanced interactions, better understanding of contexts, and providing more personalized responses. It has also stimulated discussions around consciousness, cognition, and ethics in AI, pushing the boundaries of what AI can achieve in replicating human intelligence.

Despite its historical significance in artificial intelligence, the Turing Test has faced criticism for its potential superficiality, as it measures only the machine's ability to mimic human responses, not genuine understanding or consciousness. Critics also point out cultural biases and argue that successful mimicry does not equate to intelligence or comprehension, as illustrated by thought experiments like the Chinese Room (Roberts 2016). The Chinese Room argument asserts that a computer mimicking an understanding of language is akin to a person mechanically manipulating symbols in a language they do not comprehend.

Furthermore, advancements in AI have led to systems that can pass limited forms of the test without demonstrating broad, human-like intelligence, prompting debates on the need for more comprehensive and multimodal testing criteria.

Additionally, a universally agreed-upon standard for passing the Turing Test does not exist, leading to arguments that the test should incorporate multi-modal communication forms, like visual and auditory signals, to comprehensively assess an AI's human-like abilities. The absence of a standardized approach to conducting the Turing Test has resulted in publicized assertions of "passing" the test, which are subsequently debunked or challenged (Norvig 2023).

In recent research (Jones 2023), investigators discovered that GPT-4, the newest iteration of ChatGPT, succeeded in only 41% of the tests, falling below the chance level and the 63% baseline established by human participants. Due to these results, researchers continue to assert the relevance of the Turing Test for evaluating naturalistic communication and deception despite its acknowledged limitations in measuring intelligence.

The Current Approach

Thanks to advancements in machine learning and increased computational power, AI systems have started addressing the challenge of context-aware conversations. State-of-the-art models like ChatGPT can retain conversational context, enabling more coherent and relevant dialogues. These developments indicate that AI is approaching the ability to engage in more human-like interactions. The focus has shifted from mimicking human-like behavior to utility, efficiency, and precision in specialized tasks.

Human evaluators also play a crucial role in assessing the models' practicality, safety, fairness, and cultural sensitivity. Additionally, tests are conducted to ensure these models can creatively respond to new situations they were not explicitly trained on (zero-shot evaluation). These methods help determine how effectively and safely these AI models can be used in real-world applications, ensuring they are reliable, unbiased, and capable of understanding and responding appropriately in diverse situations (Norouzi 2023).

In financial applications, however, risks still exist around reliable decision-making. As AI tools take on sensitive roles in trading, rigorous testing is crucial. Evaluating real-world performance across diverse situations, not just conversational tasks, will reveal strengths and limitations not captured by the current framework.

These evaluation techniques open the door to more specific human and machine intelligence comparisons. To fully grasp these comparisons, we must first introduce the concepts of narrow AI, general AI, superintelligence, and technological singularity.

THE HIERARCHICAL LEVELS OF ARTIFICIAL INTELLIGENCE

Narrow or Weak AI

This type of AI represents a highly specialized level of artificial intelligence designed to excel in specific functions while lacking broader applicability. For instance, a spam filter in an email system, adept at distinguishing between spam and legitimate messages, is a quintessential example of narrow AI. It performs this task with remarkable precision but is constrained to this singular function.

Similarly, advanced language models like ChatGPT, while sophisticated in processing and generating human-like text, fall under narrow AI as their expertise is confined to language and coding-related tasks.

They can develop coherent narratives, answer queries, and even mimic conversational styles. However, their capabilities are limited to their training domain without the broader cognitive understanding that characterizes more advanced forms of AI.

Likewise, quantitative models in finance fall under narrow AI. These algorithms can rapidly scan vast datasets and identify trading opportunities through pattern recognition. Nevertheless, they lack a generalized understanding of broader contexts or events that may impact trading decisions.

Today's AI systems are experts only within their narrow domains. Algorithms demonstrate stunning accuracy and speed at specialized tasks like spotting patterns in data. They even outperform people on specific functions, but they cannot adapt or transfer understanding to other situations that do not match their training. Current AI excels when problems closely align with programmed parameters—but falls short when facing unpredictable external changes or the need for general critical thinking. This divide explains how AI can be at once brilliant within specific applications while still limited in broad applicability.

Artificial General Intelligence (AGI)

AGI is the hypothetical concept of a system with the breadth and adaptability of human cognition, capable of understanding concepts, applying knowledge to unfamiliar situations, and reasoning as humans do. The idea of AGI has been popularized through fictional depictions of AI, like the character Data in Star Trek, who demonstrates self-awareness and mastery across intellectual domains at the human level. AGI represents the ultimate ambition of AI researchers to replicate artificial intelligence with the generalized capabilities of human minds.

However, despite steady progress in AI, current systems are limited to narrow applications and lack the fluid reasoning and problem-solving skills theorized in AGI. Recreating human intelligence's complex consciousness and general adaptability remains actively researched but still elusive in practice. The concept of AGI (Artificial General Intelligence), often regarded as the holy grail in the field, drives and inspires progress in AI. Researchers aspire to someday close the divide between human and artificial intelligence.

If achieved, AGI could enable fully autonomous AI traders. Empowered with versatile intelligence comparable to humans, these systems could independently develop trading strategies while accounting for many macro- and micro-economic variables. Rather than following rigid programmatic rules, AGI traders would make intuitive judgments—backed by immense data processing—about when to enter or exit positions.

These AI traders could even manipulate markets by coordinating strategies. The rise of AGI in finance could reshape markets from quant trading to investment banking. Though still hypothetical, the possibilities illuminate why achieving artificial general intelligence remains the "holy grail" for researchers across domains.

Superintelligence

Artificial superintelligence (ASI) is a speculative advanced form of AI that vastly exceeds human intelligence in every conceivable way—problem-solving, creativity, emotional intelligence, and social awareness. A hypothetical example would be a superintelligent AI that could solve complex global challenges like climate change or poverty in a few days. The concept is often linked to the idea of the "technological singularity," a theoretical point in time when the capabilities of AI grow exponentially, becoming uncontrollable and irreversible, potentially leading to unforeseen consequences for humanity.

The Technological Singularity

The "technological singularity" refers to the hypothetical time when technological growth accelerates beyond human control due to the advent of superintelligent AI. The story says that as AI systems recursively improve themselves, their intelligence will snowball into artificial superintelligence that irrevocably surpasses human-level cognition. This runaway superintelligent AI could theoretically lead to paradigm-shifting innovations that deeply transform economies, infrastructure, medicine, transportation, and humanity. Nevertheless, the singularity also risks rapidly outpacing the human ability to steer its trajectory. This event horizon concept thus signifies radical uncertainty—we may gain immense progress, but perhaps at the cost of human agency and stability. However, the details of if, when, and how this hypothetical event may unfold remain speculative.

Critical Aspects of the Technological Singularity

♦ Exponential Growth: The singularity is often associated with the idea that technological progress, especially in AI, is accelerating and will continue exponentially. It is sometimes visualized using Moore's Law, which observes the doubling of transistors on a microchip approximately every two years.

♦ Artificial Superintelligence (ASI): The singularity posits that once we develop AI that surpasses human intelligence, this AI will be capable of improving itself or creating even more advanced AI. This recursive self-improvement could lead to an intelligence explosion, making ASI vastly superior to human intelligence.

♦ Unpredictability: The singularity represents a horizon beyond which outcomes are hard to predict. How a hypothetical ASI would behave, its decisions, and its impact on society are all uncertain.

♦ Transformation of Society: The singularity could lead to profound changes in human life, from economics and politics to culture and interpersonal relationships.

Potential Outcomes and Scenarios

♦ Utopian Visions: The singularity could usher in a new era of prosperity, with ASI solving many of humanity's pressing problems, such as disease, poverty, and environmental degradation.

♦ Dystopian Concerns: Alternatively, the ASI could become uncontrollable, leading to human extinction or a scenario where humans are subjugated.

♦ Merging with Machines: Another perspective suggests that humans might integrate with technology, enhancing our cognitive and physical abilities, thus preventing a clear distinction between humans and machines.

♦ Economic Disruption: Rapid advancements could lead to significant job displacements, economic inequalities, and societal upheavals.

Criticisms and Skepticism

While the concept of the singularity is prevalent in some tech and futurist circles, it is also met with skepticism:

- Overly Optimistic Projections: Predictions like Moore's Law cannot continue indefinitely, and technological growth has physical limits.
- Complexity: Intelligence, particularly human intelligence, may be too complex to arise using AI algorithms, making the creation of ASI a far-off goal.
- Unfounded Predictions: Forecasting specific timelines for such a profound event is speculative at best.

The emergence of artificial superintelligence could fundamentally transform finance as machine cognition surpasses human capabilities. Self-improving algorithmic trading systems may accelerate markets and efficiency beyond imagined frontiers. New industries springing from ASI breakthroughs could also spur growth. However, the speed and complexity of ASI-directed markets could also overwhelm regulators, inducing market failures or crashes.

After understanding our current position in the narrow stage of AI development, we can provide a clear framework for drawing comparisons between human and artificial intelligence, allowing us to learn how these distinct forms of intelligence function, interact, and contrast.

Comparison of Human and Artificial Intelligence

Numerous instances illustrate how artificial intelligence has exceeded human capabilities in specific fields:

- Chess: Deep Blue vs. Garry Kasparov: In 1997, IBM's Deep Blue defeated world chess champion Garry Kasparov. Deep Blue excelled in computational power despite lacking humans' intuitive and strategic thinking.
- Jeopardy!: IBM Watson: Watson's 2011 victory showcased AI's ability to understand natural language. The nature of "Jeopardy!" questions often involve puns, nuances, and intricate language structures that are typically difficult for computers to understand.

◆ AlphaGo and Go: DeepMind's AlphaGo defeated world champion Lee Sedol in the game of Go, an achievement previously believed to be decades in the future.

◆ Poker: AI advancements were also evident in poker, a game of imperfect information. In 2017, an AI called Libratus defeated four professional poker players in Texas Hold 'em, demonstrating AI's capacity to make decisions based on incomplete information and guesswork, a significant step beyond mere computational power.

◆ Algorithmic Trading: AI systems have been widely used in high-frequency trading, where they analyze vast amounts of financial data at high speeds to make trading decisions. These systems can identify arbitrage opportunities that disappear before humans get a chance to react.

Despite these results, humans demonstrate remarkable adaptability, learning from limited examples and generalizing this knowledge across various domains. This inherent flexibility starkly contrasts with AI, which, while advanced in specific tasks, requires extensive datasets for training and often struggles with tasks beyond its programmed scope.

IBM's Deep Blue, Watson, and DeepMind's AlphaGo lack a robust mental model and a comprehensive representation of reality, making these systems susceptible to unexpected strategies that exploit gaps in their training and algorithms.

For example, years after AlphaGo's sweep of the ancient board game Go, amateur player Kellin Pelrine defeated one of the world's top-ranked AI systems in Go in 2023. Without direct aid from other programs, Pelrine exploited a strategic flaw in the AI system to clinch victory in 14 out of 15 games. This win used a plan conceived using a computer program to detect blind spots in AI training, highlighting a typical AI weakness (Waters 2023).

While narrow AI has achieved superhuman proficiency in specific domains, general human intelligence still maintains decisive advantages in adaptability, generalizability, creativity, and emotional awareness. Humans exhibit a versatility to learn and thrive in multifaceted situations. We forge understanding through data, experiential wisdom, and emotional maturity. Recent examples illustrate that even young talents can outmaneuver cutting-edge AI by exploiting their lack of understanding. Integrating human and machine intelligence strengths will likely catalyze the best outcomes.

From Machine Learning to Deep Learning: The Rise of AI Models

The pursuit of replicating human intelligence in machines has been a driving force for innovators throughout history, from Aristotle's systematic logic to Descartes' conception of bodies as machines—laying conceptual seeds for today's AI. In 1956, John McCarthy officially named the field at the Dartmouth Workshop, setting in motion a project aimed at mimicking language, reasoning, and problem-solving in machines, ideally during that summer.

More than 60 years later, AI has not yet fulfilled these ambitious goals. Despite periods of exaggerated expectations and subsequent setbacks, the discipline has advanced significantly, from encoding human knowledge in symbolic rules to developing modern machine-learning programs that can learn from data directly.

THE SYMBOLIC APPROACH

In the mid-1900s, AI pioneers like Marvin Minsky and John McCarthy led the Symbolic approach. This approach encodes human knowledge into machines with symbols. From the 1950s to 1990s, milestones like Logic Theorist (that proved mathematical theorems) and IBM's Deep Blue beating chess master Garry Kasparov created optimism.

However, this approach struggled with messy real-world data. Despite some structure, it could not match human intelligence. Progress began to slow, periodically producing "AI winters," periods marked by drastic declines in funding and interest as initial optimism faded.

Thankfully, the rise of big data, new algorithms, and more potent computers enabled machine learning in recent years. This AI analyzes data to find patterns instead of using pre-set symbolic rules.

MACHINE LEARNING: THE FOUNDATION

The origins of Machine Learning trace back to 1957 with Frank Rosenblatt's invention of the perceptron, a precursor to today's machine learning models that mimicked decision-making processes akin to human thinking. In parallel, Arthur Samuel's innovative work in the 1950s and '60s demonstrated machines' ability to learn from experiences. Significantly, the backpropagation algorithm developed later allowed these models to learn from mistakes and improve over time (Werbos 1990).

Perceptron   The perceptron works by receiving multiple input signals, each assigned a weight signifying its importance. The perceptron processes these inputs based on their weighted sum and decides whether to "fire." If the sum exceeds a certain threshold, the perceptron outputs a signal; otherwise, it remains inactive. This simple yet powerful mechanism allows it to learn and make decisions. While perceptrons introduced the foundational concept of a simple neural model, more complex networks with additional layers of perceptual nodes or "neurons" radically enhanced learning capabilities. These multilayered neural networks form the basis of modern AI, particularly machine learning.

What Is Machine Learning?

Machine learning (ML) represents a specific branch within the broader field of AI that concentrates on devising algorithms that empower computers to derive insights from data and base their decisions on these insights. Rather than being directly programmed for a specific task, a machine learning model uses statistical techniques to discover patterns in data and make predictions or decisions based on them.

Machine learning implementations are typically divided into three main types: Supervised, Unsupervised, and Reinforcement Learning.

Supervised Learning   This approach is akin to a pupil acquiring knowledge with the supervision of an instructor, where the "teacher" is the labeled dataset providing examples of correct outcomes. The algorithm repeatedly generates predictions using the input data and receives corrections from the dataset, much like a student learning from mistakes and feedback. Over time, the algorithm becomes more proficient in mapping inputs to the correct outputs, improving its predictions or classifications. This makes supervised learning highly applicable for forecasting future outcomes based on historical examples.

This method is prevalent in applications like image recognition and prediction tasks, where algorithms learn to classify input into various categories based on the labeled examples they have been trained on. With increased exposure to data and ongoing learning, these models can reach heightened levels of precision.

Supervised models, when applied to finance, are surprisingly ineffective. Supervised learning assumes that the world will continue to behave as it did in the past (stationarity). However, this assumption is only reasonable within very short horizons because investors continuously adapt and learn, rendering past data less predictive. As a result, the only relevant data for these models is that from the immediate past, which represents the current market behavior. This continuous adaptation by investors results in a chronic shortage of long-term, stable data to train these models effectively. Consequently, supervised learning models often fail to account for structural changes in market dynamics over time, as they are perpetually playing catch-up with the latest market trends.

Unsupervised Learning   Unsupervised learning can be likened to students exploring a new concept independently without specific guidance or correct answers. Here, the algorithm is given data without labels or specified outcomes and must find structure and patterns. It is about discovering and identifying hidden features in data, clustering similar data points together, or reducing the dimensionality of the data to understand its structure better.

This form of learning is convenient for exploratory data analysis, customer segmentation, and complex scenarios where the relationships or patterns are not initially apparent. It allows algorithms to uncover hidden correlations without needing predefined labels or categories.

Unsupervised learning is constantly used in financial applications when using factor models to understand how different stocks move together. In this context, unsupervised learning algorithms, like Principal Component Analysis (PCA) or cluster analysis, are employed to uncover these hidden factors.

Reinforcement Learning (RL)   Consider reinforcement learning analogous to learning a new skill through trial and error, where the learner receives feedback through rewards or penalties. The "learner" is an agent that makes decisions, takes actions, and learns optimal behavior by interacting with its environment to achieve specific objectives. Each decision has consequences, and the agent adjusts its strategy to maximize the cumulative reward over time.

This approach is instrumental in dynamic environments where the algorithm must make a series of decisions that depend on the current state and its previous actions. It is used in robotics, video games, and autonomous vehicles, where improving strategy and adapting to new situations are crucial. Reinforcement learning holds intriguing potential in finance, offering a method for deploying agents capable of trading in the financial market. However, its practical application faces significant hurdles.

Reinforcement learning requires substantial data for experimentation, but historical data is only relevant within short horizons, as investors constantly adapt to market patterns. These models need to extensively explore the strategy space before developing profitable approaches. However, the market dynamics may have changed by the time they start generating profits. Consequently, despite its theoretical promise, the deployment of RL in financial settings has been limited, as achieving consistent, real-world effectiveness remains a formidable challenge.

These techniques, in their modern form, are powered by neural networks.

Neural Networks (NN) An NN is a series of computer instructions founded on a mathematical model that aims to identify underlying patterns within a dataset by simulating the processes resembling those of the human brain. It is a system of interconnected nodes (neurons) working together to process complex data inputs, learn from them, and make decisions or predictions. These networks can adapt and improve their performance as they are exposed to more data, making them powerful tools for various applications, from image and speech recognition to predictive analytics. Rather than relying on rigid human-crafted rules, they self-organize to master these tasks.

Inspired by early neural network models, deep learning leverages modern computational power and vast datasets to train huge, complex neural nets with more layers and parameters. These multi-layered networks can learn sophisticated feature representations.

DEEP LEARNING

Deep learning is the technique of training and deploying artificial neural networks with many layers (hence deep) to recognize patterns and make decisions. While a single-layer neural network can provide rough predictions, additional hidden layers can help to refine those predictions. Adding layers makes networks easier to train compared to growing shallow networks. Deep learning has become indispensable where exceedingly high accuracy or intuiting intricate patterns from data is requisite. Deep neural networks represent the state of the art in machine learning, and there are several types of deep neural networks, each appropriate for different tasks.

Convolutional Neural Networks (CNNs)   CNNs, designed for image processing, have revolutionized fields like medical imaging, facial recognition, and autonomous vehicles. Their ability to efficiently process and interpret visual data enables applications ranging from diagnosing diseases from X-rays to powering the vision systems in self-driving cars.

Recurrent Neural Networks (RNNs)   RNNs are artificial neural networks designed explicitly for processing sequential data. RNNs' ability to maintain a hidden state or memory of previous inputs in the sequence sets them apart from traditional feed-forward neural networks. This memory allows RNNs to capture temporal dependencies and relationships within the data, making them well-suited for tasks involving sequences, such as time series analysis, natural language processing (NLP), and speech recognition.

RNNs are widely used in NLP tasks like language modeling, text generation, and machine translation. Their ability to handle variable-length sequences makes them valuable in these applications. For instance, in machine translation, RNNs can take a sentence in one language and generate a corresponding sentence in another.

However, traditional RNNs have some limitations. They can struggle with capturing long-range dependencies in sequences, which can result in the "vanishing gradient" problem, hindering their performance on tasks that require remembering information from distant past inputs.

Long Short-Term Memory Networks (LSTMs)   LSTMs address these limitations. LSTMs are a type of RNN with more complex memory cells, allowing them to capture long-range dependencies more effectively. Due to their capacity to effectively manage sequential data, they have emerged as a critical element in numerous deep learning applications, enhancing overall performance.

Generative Adversarial Networks (GANs) GANs are known for generating realistic images and videos. They are widely used in creating art, deepfake videos, and enhancing low-resolution pictures. In fashion and design, GANs help in creating new designs and patterns.

Autoencoders Autoencoders are primarily used for data compression and denoising. They are vital in reducing data dimensionality and help in efficient data storage and noise reduction in images and signals.

Generative AI Models These models, including GPTs (Generative Pre-trained Transformers), are primarily used in content generation. They have applications in creating textual content, from writing articles to generating code and even creating new forms of entertainment like games and music.

Large Language Models (LLMs) LLMs like GPT-3 are pivotal in understanding language and generating texts, and they are used in chatbots, content creation, and language translation services. They are transforming customer service, education, and entertainment by providing more human-like interactions and content. We will discuss LLMs in depth in the next chapter.

The Rise of Deep Learning
Several factors have converged over recent years to catapult deep learning methodologies to the forefront of artificial intelligence. First, the fast growth of digital data has provided the critical raw material. From social media platforms to internet-connected sensors, vast datasets are generated continuously, enabling models to learn complex patterns. Concurrently, graphical processing units (GPUs) have unlocked transformative computational speeds—their parallelized architecture perfectly suits the matrix calculations integral to neural networks. Initially designed for video game visuals, GPUs can

train advanced models thousands of times faster than traditional processors.

Equally importantly, improved algorithms and accessible tools now facilitate implementation. Seminal advances like generative adversarial networks, attention mechanisms, and transformers have enhanced learning across computer vision, speech, and language without overfitting. Meanwhile, open-source frameworks like TensorFlow and PyTorch have lowered the barriers to education and development. Moving forward, deep learning forms the backbone of these new systems, enabling broad AI progress across industries and applications.

Deep learning models outperform traditional algorithms in many tasks, including image and speech recognition, prediction, and natural language processing. Their ability to process unstructured data, like images and text, and extract meaningful patterns is unparalleled. This versatility and superior performance have made them the go-to choice for many AI applications.

The ascension of deep learning in artificial intelligence has set the stage for the emergence and success of large language models. These sophisticated models, exemplified by ChatGPT, are a direct outcome of the advancements in deep learning techniques and computational power. As deep learning continues to evolve, it promises to enhance the capabilities of LLMs further, continually pushing the boundaries of what is possible in AI and finance.

Summary

In this chapter, we covered the basics of artificial intelligence and built the conceptual framework to explore its financial applications. We learned about the components of AI systems, from hardware and software to algorithms and neural networks. We discussed the different types of machine-learning models, including supervised, unsupervised, and reinforcement learning, that enable computers to learn from data.

You also learned about the levels of artificial intelligence, from narrow AI that excels at specific tasks to hypothetical concepts like artificial general intelligence and technological singularity. We compared human cognition and current AI capabilities, noting how machines have surpassed humans in certain domains while lacking flexibility and generalizability.

Tracing the history of AI, you understand how the field progressed from early symbolic approaches to the current dominance of deep learning techniques. We covered different neural network architectures that have driven progress in computer vision, natural language processing, and other AI applications. This set the foundation for introducing large language models that can generate remarkably human-like text.

As AI capabilities continue advancing, understanding these foundations will equip you to see the connections between AI and finance. You will be able to grasp how AI is applied in areas ranging from sentiment analysis of news to high-frequency algorithmic trading. Going forward, the transformational impacts of AI on the finance industry will become more apparent.

Coming Up Next

The next chapter explores the transformative impact of LLMs in natural language processing (NLP) and generative AI. It discusses the foundational aspects of NLP, the generative AI advancements, and their capabilities in generating human-like text and understanding context. The chapter addresses critical challenges in NLP, the role of generative AI in creativity, and LLMs' benefits and ethical considerations.

Check Your Understanding Questions

What is artificial intelligence?

◆ Describe the basic concept of AI and its primary purpose in technology.

What are the two fundamental aspects of intelligence discussed in the chapter?

◆ Identify and briefly describe the two aspects of intelligence highlighted as crucial for understanding AI.

According to Howard Gardner's theory, please list and describe the types of human intelligence.

♦ Name and briefly explain each type of intelligence proposed by Howard Gardner.

How do computers and AI currently measure up against human intelligence?

♦ Examine both the capabilities and constraints of AI in comparison to human cognitive abilities.

What are the different types of machine learning, and how do they work?

♦ Define and give examples of supervised, unsupervised, and reinforcement learning.

How does deep learning differ from traditional machine learning?

♦ Explain what deep learning is and how it represents an evolution of machine learning.

What are some ethical considerations and limitations of AI?

♦ Identify and elaborate on at least three ethical considerations or limitations in developing and implementing AI.

What is the Turing Test, and what are its criticisms?

♦ Describe the Turing Test, and discuss why some believe it may not be an adequate measure of AI intelligence.

What are the hierarchical levels of AI, and what distinguishes them?

♦ Explain the concepts of Narrow AI, General AI, and Superintelligence, noting key differences.

What recent advancements have led to the rise of AI models?

♦ Identify and describe recent technological or theoretical advancements that have significantly contributed to the development of AI.

CHAPTER 3

Large Language Models:
A Game Changer

Large language models (LLMs) are the most sophisticated form of artificial intelligence we have so far. The technology powers models like ChatGPT, allowing them to understand and generate nuanced, human-like language and solve tasks like coding and following instructions. As LLMs become more advanced, their disruptive impact on quantitative analysis and algorithmic trading seems imminent. LLMs can analyze earnings reports, extract data, generate investment research notes, and even provide individualized stock recommendations tailored to investors' goals and risk tolerance. Understanding this technology will help you leverage and keep pace with AI's rapid progress.

This chapter explores the transformative role of large language models. The first section, natural language processing (NLP), lays the foundation by explaining how computers understand and process human language. It sets the stage for understanding the complexity of language tasks that LLMs manage to perform.

The second section, generative AI, expands on the capabilities of AI systems to create new, original content, a leap forward from traditional, rule-based approaches. It illustrates the evolution from simple language processing to generating coherent and contextually relevant content.

Finally, the third section, LLMs, focuses on these sophisticated models at the forefront of NLP and generative AI. LLMs like GPT-3 have revolutionized the field by demonstrating an unprecedented ability to generate human-like text, pushing the boundaries of what is possible in machine-generated language and content creation.

The core concepts covered in this chapter—natural language processing, generative AI, and the breakthrough capabilities of large language models—establish an essential foundation. Understanding both the tremendous potential and current limitations of this technology is crucial. In later chapters, we build on these fundamentals to explore practical applications of large language models in quantitative analysis, algorithmic trading, and other areas of finance. Learning about their inner workings will provide insight into deploying current models and acquiring the foundational knowledge to adapt fluently as the field rapidly evolves.

What Is Natural Language Processing?

Natural language processing stands at the convergence of linguistics, computer science, and artificial intelligence, embodying a field with multiple facets. Its objective is to equip machines with the capability to comprehend, interpret, produce, and react to human language in a meaningful and beneficial manner. NLP seeks to solve the complex problem of making computers understand human language. Unlike programming languages, designed to be unambiguous and easily interpreted by machines, human language is full of nuance, context, and ambiguity. NLP uses various techniques to translate this complexity into formats that computers can understand. This section explores NLP's key concepts, methodologies, and applications, providing a comprehensive overview of this fascinating and rapidly evolving field.

NLP has invaluable applications in financial domains like stock market analysis and quantitative investing. Tasks like sentiment analysis of news articles, earnings call transcripts, and social media can provide unique insights into investor psychology and future stock movements. NLP techniques can also automatically extract key statistics, business metrics, and management commentary from lengthy earnings reports and regulatory filings.

CRITICAL CHALLENGES IN NLP

There are several critical challenges in NLP. One key challenge is ambiguity. For example, the word "bat" can mean a flying mammal or a piece of baseball equipment, depending on the context. NLP systems must decipher such ambiguities to understand language accurately.

Another challenge is the distinction between syntax and semantics. Syntax focuses on grammatical structure, while semantics deals with meaning. An NLP system might correctly parse the syntax of a sentence but misinterpret its semantic meaning, leading to misunderstandings.

Sarcasm and sentiment pose additional hurdles. Detecting sarcasm or irony, which often depends on subtle cues and context, is particularly challenging for NLP systems. These systems may struggle to differentiate between a positive statement and a sarcastic remark conveying the opposite sentiment.

Domain-specific vocabulary poses an additional challenge. Financial texts are filled with niche terms, acronyms, and numbers with little meaning to general NLP models. Adapting these systems to understand concepts like asset valuation, risk factors, and earnings projections remains an active area of research. Interpreting the ambiguous language frequently found in policy announcements and central bank statements also confounds algorithms.

CORE TECHNIQUES AND ALGORITHMS OF NLP

NLP employs diverse techniques and algorithms to automatically interpret, process, analyze, and generate human language. Some core techniques include tokenization, entity recognition, and machine translation.

Tokenization

This method is the foundational step in NLP, where text is segmented into smaller units called tokens. These tokens are often individual words or sub-words, providing a base for further linguistic analysis. This process is critical for understanding the structure and meaning of language, as it allows algorithms to process and analyze text in manageable chunks, paving the way for more complex operations. Consider the phrase "AI predicts." Tokenization breaks this down into three tokens: ["AI", "predicts", "."]. These three chunks can be processed for tasks like named entity recognition or next-word prediction. We will explore tokenization in depth in Chapter 5, including handling multi-word tokens like proper nouns and the role of tokens in training large language models.

Named Entity Recognition (NER)

NER is a method that locates and categorizes specific elements in text into pre-established groups, such as names, organizations, and locations. For instance, in a news article, NER would pinpoint the names of people, places, firms, and dates or events. NER is essential for extracting useful information from large volumes of text, aiding in tasks like data retrieval and content organization. In the sentence, "Leonardo da Vinci was born in Italy," NER recognizes "Leonardo da Vinci" as a person and "Italy" as a location.

NER has valuable applications for analyzing unstructured textual data related to investing and the stock market. NER can automatically extract entity types like company names, executives, locations, products, subsidiaries, and more from earnings call transcripts, business news articles, financial reports, and other texts.

Investors can leverage NER systems to parse thousands of 10-K and 10-Q filings to rapidly locate mentions of key organization names, executive leaders, production facilities, or operating locations. Tracking these entities over time for a firm could reveal insightful trends—for example, frequently expanding to new cities or opening factories in foreign nations. This may signal a geographical growth strategy.

Similarly, NER can pinpoint emerging affiliations or terminations between companies and partners in analysis. For example, mentioning a supplier name or subsidiary drop-off may signify moved operations or a severed relationship. NER provides efficient wide-scale entity monitoring to accelerate the discovery of these patterns from voluminous text data.

In earnings call transcripts, NER identifies speaker names and roles in how executive mood or focus shifts over time. Along with organizations and people, accurately tracking products, competitors, operations, and global issues touching the business creates a detailed picture to inform investment decisions.

Machine Translation

This process involves automatically converting text from one language into another. Machine translation systems like Google Translate capture the essence of the original text using complex statistical or neural network algorithms and render it in a different target language. This makes global communication much more accessible; for example, we can translate a Spanish news article into English. There are many approaches to machine translation, including rule-based (structuring linguistic rules), statistical (analyzing patterns in large bilingual text corpora), and neural systems (using deep learning models). The field has progressed rapidly, with neural machine translation rivaling human capabilities for some language pairs.

Text Summarization

This method condenses lengthy documents into shorter versions, capturing the main points or essential information. It is widely used in summarizing news articles, research papers, and long reports, ensuring readers can grasp critical concepts without reading the entire text. Text summarization is very helpful when dealing with long firms' filings, as it allows us to focus on the core information and discard the rest. The ability to quickly distill essential information from extensive financial documents, such as earnings reports or SEC filings, means faster and more informed investment decisions.

NLP APPLICATIONS

In Natural Language Processing (NLP), blending advanced technology and human language has led to remarkable applications that are reshaping our daily interactions with machines and digital systems.

Search Engines

NLP revolutionizes search engines' operations, enabling them to understand and process user queries. This ability leads to more effective and accurate search results, providing users with information that closely matches their intent and context.

Chatbots

NLP transforms chatbots into more intuitive and responsive tools. They can understand nuances in human language, allowing for smoother, more human-like conversations and greatly enhancing user experience in customer service and support.

NLP-powered chatbots could allow retail investing platforms to provide customer service support to individual investors at an immense scale. Rather than employing large call centers, users' common questions around account balances, order statuses, tax forms, etc., could be fielded through conversational bots. These bots empower users to self-serve information, reducing overhead costs. Even complex queries about market events or trading strategies could be addressed through machine learning models, providing human-like personalized guidance.

However, today's NLP chatbots cannot match human versatility and judgment for handling nuanced, context-heavy dialog. Deploying bots prematurely could damage customers' trust and experience if bots provide incorrect or tone-deaf answers on sensitive financial topics. Their reasoning is also opaque compared to humans, making it harder to audit and improve responses.

Thus, fintech firms need caution in adopting chatbots—likely supplementing rather than entirely replacing human agents in the short term. Tight oversight of bot training data and functionality is necessary to avoid compliance or ethical pitfalls around investment guidance.

Sentiment Analysis

Through NLP, businesses can effectively analyze vast amounts of text data, like customer reviews or social media posts, to extract public sentiment. This technique provides valuable insights into customer preferences and market trends. In later chapters, we will explore how sentiment analysis can be used to develop investment strategies.

Speech Recognition

NLP is integral to the functionality of voice-activated assistants. It enables these assistants to interpret and respond to voice commands accurately, making technology more accessible and convenient.

Speech recognition and NLP are making major strides toward usable voice interfaces for financial services. Hands-free, voice-driven navigation of banking, trading, and market data analysis could greatly enhance finance professionals' productivity on desktop or mobile. Yet today's solutions still have limitations.

In wealth management, an advisor presenting complex product guidance to clients could leverage voice commands to instantly pull up relevant performance charts, prospectuses, or account tools, freeing client focus. Advanced speech AI may someday act as a digital co-pilot, helping construct personalized investment plans through conversing dialog as meetings unfold.

For active traders, verbal interfaces facilitate faster order execution versus manual UIs built for tap and click. Requesting real-time quotes, analysis, or order placement through speech as market events unfold enables quicker reactions.

Generative AI: The Art of Digital Creation

Generative AI is a subset of AI focused on creating new, original content rather than purely analyzing data or making predictions. Unlike other types of AI designed to forecast, generative AI aims to produce something novel, be it text, images, music, code, or complex scenarios. It is akin to a digital artist, trained to analyze or interpret existing works and create new masterpieces.

In finance, generative AI's ability to imagine realistic scenarios is helpful when envisioning potential future trajectories for stock returns, as we will see in later chapters. Generative AI may also compose detailed earnings guidance conditioned on emergent geopolitical tensions, M&A deals, or disruptive product launches. Analysts can quickly vet and refine hundreds of persuasive scenarios to game-plan responses versus manually enumerating assumptions today.

The generative AI process begins with the learning phase, a critical stage where the AI model undergoes training. During this period, the algorithm is exposed to a plethora of existing content, ranging from text documents and images to more complex data like human behaviors or weather patterns. Like an aspiring artist devoting years to studying classic pieces, generative AI models undergo extensive training on vast datasets before producing anything. In the case of a text generator, this would mean ingesting millions of news articles, books, and web pages to learn intricate linguistic patterns.

However, the algorithm does not just memorize this content; it learns to understand its underlying patterns and structures. This understanding is encapsulated in what is known as a statistical model—a set of mathematical functions encoding its knowledge. Think of this model as the artist's creative intuition, a mental framework guiding their endeavors. It is a set of rules and guidelines, albeit complex ones, that the algorithm has inferred from the data it was trained on.

Once trained, generative AI goes beyond replicating what it has seen. It uses its statistical model to generate new content exhibiting features of human creativity that, while based on its training, is original and novel. It is like a trained artist who starts creating their unique pieces after years of studying the classics. The classics influence these new pieces, but rather than mere imitations, they are original works reflecting the statistical model learned.

One of generative AI's most intriguing aspects is the balance between novelty and coherence. The algorithm aims to produce new and meaningful content, which is easier said than done. Too much reliance on the statistical model might result in outputs that are predictable and lack originality. On the other hand, straying too far from the model could lead to random and nonsensical content. It is a delicate balance, like an artist combining innovative expression and understandable communication.

THE MULTIFACETED OUTPUTS OF GENERATIVE AI

Generative AI is a versatile creator capable of producing a wide array of outputs depending on the type of input it receives. These models can learn the joint probability distribution of text, images, and videos. This adaptability pushes the boundaries of the definition of creativity. There are many possibilities depending on the input type:

When the Input Is an Image

♦ Text: Generative AI can produce descriptive text when fed an image. This text could be as simple as identifying the objects in the image or as complex as generating a narrative or story based on the scene depicted. The AI uses its trained statistical model to interpret the visual elements and translate them into coherent and contextually relevant text.

♦ Image: Generative AI can also transform an input image into another. This transformation could involve altering the style of the image, like converting a photograph into an impressionist painting or modifying its content, such as changing the background of a portrait.

♦ Video: Extending its capabilities further, generative AI can even produce a video based on an input image. For instance, it might animate a still picture, adding motion to a previously static scene. The AI uses its understanding of the elements in the image to generate plausible and coherent movement, bringing the picture to life.

When the Input Is Text

♦ Text: generative AI can produce new text output when provided with text as input. This exercise could range from generating a poem based on a single line to creating a full-length article based on a headline. The AI uses its understanding of language structure, context, and semantics to produce relevant and original text.

♦ Image: Generative AI can also convert text descriptions into visual images. For example, given the text "a serene beach at sunset," the AI could generate an image visually representing this description. It interprets the adjectives, nouns, and the overall context to create a visual output that aligns with the textual input.

♦ Audio: Audio is another frontier for generative AI. It can produce audio content given a text input, such as converting a written script into spoken words using text-to-speech technology. It can even generate music based on textual descriptions, like creating a soothing melody described as "calm and peaceful."

Generative AI is not merely a tool for analysis or prediction but a creative entity capable of generating diverse and novel content. This toolset includes large language models specializing in text generation, among other output forms like images and decisions. Through advanced training processes, generative AI develops statistical models that act as its creative intuition, enabling it to produce outputs that blur the lines between machine-generated content and human creativity.

Large Language Models

One of the most recent transformative developments is the emergence of large language models (LLMs). These models, characterized by their immense size and unparalleled capabilities, redefine what machines can achieve when understanding and generating human language.

WHAT ARE LLMs?

At their core, LLMs are a deep learning model designed to understand, generate, and interact using natural language. LLMs are trained on massive text datasets, enabling them to recognize language patterns, nuances, and intricacies. The term "large" in their designation is quite apt; these models comprise hundreds of billions of parameters, positioning them among the most advanced AI models.

LLMs, like the GPT (Generative Pre-trained Transformer) series by the OpenAI company, use a type of neural network called transformers. These transformers are adept at handling sequences, making them ideal for language tasks. The models are first pre-trained on vast datasets, absorbing information from books, articles, websites, and more. This pre-training phase equips them with a broad understanding of language. They are then fine-tuned on specific tasks, enhancing their performance in targeted applications.

Their ability to understand the context sets LLMs apart from traditional language models. While earlier models could recognize words and basic structures, LLMs can grasp nuances, idioms, and cultural references. This deep understanding allows them to generate human-like text, answer complex questions, and engage in meaningful conversations. Furthermore, their vast training data means they have been exposed to many topics, making them versatile tools in various applications, including finance.

LLMs can parse market news and regulatory documents to improve search, sentiment analysis, and information extraction for investors. Their ability to synthesize market data into natural language descriptions generates useful visualizations of macro trends, industry dynamics, or investment theses. LLMs even show promise for suggesting causal hypotheses on what drives asset swings based on correlating news and price events. In later chapters, we will explore specific applications of LLMs in trading.

The benefits of large language models are manifold, offering a blend of versatility, efficiency, and accessibility unparalleled in artificial intelligence. As these models evolve, they promise to revolutionize how we interact with technology, making our lives easier, more informed, and more connected.

THE BENEFITS OF LARGE LANGUAGE MODELS: UNLOCKING THE POWER OF ADVANCED AI

Imagine having a personal assistant who helps you write emails and summarize articles, answers your questions on various topics, and even helps you learn a new language. Large language models (LLMs) like GPT-3 and GPT-4 offer these capabilities and more.

Versatility These models can perform various tasks, from generating text and code to assisting decision-making. They are the Swiss Army knife of the digital world, equipped with various tools to handle multiple challenges. For example, they can follow instructions, write code, and analyze market conditions.

Efficiency Whether automating customer service responses or generating reports, these models can perform tasks in a fraction of the time it would take a human. This efficiency allows businesses and individuals to focus on complex and creative tasks.

Accessibility LLMs democratize information by providing high-quality, reliable answers to various queries. Whether you want to generate investment ideas, seek marketing tips, or write a trading system from scratch, LLMs bring expertise to your fingertips.

Customization LLMs can be customized using fine-tuning to serve specific industries or tasks. This customization means you can have a model that understands the terminology of your field, be it healthcare, law, or finance, and provides relevant solutions.

Language Support LLMs are trained on data from various languages and cultures, making them capable of understanding and generating text in multiple languages. This capability is invaluable for global businesses and multicultural communities, as it helps bridge linguistic and cultural gaps.

Continuous Learning   The world is constantly evolving, and LLMs are also changing. These models can adapt to new information, trends, and technologies through periodic updates and fine-tuning, ensuring they remain relevant and valuable.

PROBLEMS WITH LLMs

However, LLMs are not free of errors and problems. Two significant problems are bias and hallucinations.

As large language models become increasingly integrated into our daily lives, the issue of bias within these models has come under scrutiny. From perpetuating stereotypes to misrepresenting facts, the prejudices in LLMs can have far-reaching consequences.

Bias in LLMs is a pressing issue that requires concerted efforts from researchers, developers, and policymakers alike. While it is challenging to eliminate bias, understanding its origins and consequences is the first step in mitigating its impact. As we continue to deploy LLMs in various sectors, we must address these biases to ensure that technology is an enabler rather than a barrier to social progress.

What Are Biases in LLMs?

Biases in LLMs refer to the systematic errors or prejudices these models exhibit when processing or generating text. They can affect the model's understanding of language, responses, and decision-making abilities.

Origins of Bias

- ◆ Training Data. LLMs are trained on vast datasets, often including text from the internet, books, and other sources. These datasets can contain inherent societal biases, which the model learns during training.
- ◆ Annotation Process. In supervised learning, human annotators label the data. Their personal biases can inadvertently be incorporated into the model.
- ◆ Algorithmic Factors. Some algorithms may amplify existing biases, specifically when the model is fine-tuned for specific tasks.

Consequences of Bias

- ◆ Reinforcement of Stereotypes. Biased LLMs can reinforce harmful stereotypes, leading to perpetuation rather than mitigation of social issues.

- Decision-Making. A biased model could make unfair and discriminatory application decisions like hiring or loan approval.
- Misinformation. Biased models can generate or spread misinformation, affecting public opinion and discourse.

Gender bias in translation services is an example of bias. Some language translation algorithms have tended to associate genders with certain professions. For example, translating from gender-neutral languages to gendered ones, these services might default to male pronouns for occupations like doctors and engineers, perpetuating gender stereotypes. This shortcoming reflects underlying biases in training data and the need for more nuanced algorithmic approaches.

Racial bias in sentiment analysis is another vital issue. Research has indicated that some LLMs used in sentiment analysis can display racial bias. These models have shown a propensity to associate negative sentiments more frequently with names commonly belonging to minority groups. This issue highlights the challenges in ensuring AI systems are trained on diverse and representative datasets to avoid perpetuating societal biases.

The presence of biases in large language models has significant implications for their use in investment strategies. For instance, if LLMs are employed for financial analysis or algorithmic trading, existing biases in the models could lead to distorted evaluations of companies or markets, impacting investment decisions and portfolio performance. This is particularly critical in areas like environmental, social, and governance (ESG) investing, where a nuanced understanding of social and governance issues is essential. Biased interpretations could lead to underrepresentation or misinterpreting crucial ESG factors, potentially misleading investors.

Mitigating Bias
Although the problem is not easy to solve, several measures are currently being taken:

- Transparent Algorithms. Open-sourcing algorithms allow for community-based scrutiny and correction of biases.
- Diverse Training Data. Incorporating diversity in the training data can help in reducing bias.
- Ethical Guidelines. Ethical guidelines for data annotation and model deployment can safeguard against bias.

◆ Continuous Monitoring. Regular audits of LLMs help identify and rectify biases as they emerge.

Hallucinations in Large Language Models

In LLMs like GPT-3 or GPT-4, the term "hallucinations" refers to instances where the model generates output that is factually incorrect, nonsensical, or unsupported by the input data. Imagine asking a model a historical question and receiving an answer that includes events or characters that never existed. These inaccuracies are akin to "hallucinations" because the model seems to see or interpret things that aren't there.

A clear example occurred when a lawyer used the AI assistant ChatGPT to help research precedents to cite in a legal brief. ChatGPT fabricated details of several court cases—including fake judges' names, docket numbers, court circuits, quotes, and decisions. When directly asked, it even assured the lawyer that these bogus cases were genuine. But none of these cases existed. The language model had essentially hallucinated an entire convincing string of legal precedents that never happened.

Hallucinations in large language models are a challenge. Understanding why they occur and minimizing them can go a long way in improving the reliability and usefulness of these advanced AI systems. As we continue to refine and develop LLMs, addressing the issue of hallucinations will be crucial in making them more accurate and trustworthy tools for various applications.

Why Do Hallucinations Exist? Hallucinations in LLMs can be attributed to several factors:

◆ Imperfect Training Data: No dataset is entirely error-free or bias-free. Since LLMs learn from vast amounts of data, they may inadvertently learn to replicate these inaccuracies.

◆ Model Complexity: LLMs are incredibly complex, with millions or even billions of parameters. This complexity can sometimes lead to unpredictable behavior, including the generation of hallucinated content.

◆ Lack of Ground Truth During Inference: Unlike humans, LLMs do not have a "ground truth" or a sense of real-world facts when they generate output. They rely solely on statistical patterns learned during training.

♦ Overfitting: Sometimes, a model may perform exceptionally well on its training data but poorly on new, unseen data. This over-specialization can result in hallucinations when the model encounters inputs that differ from its training data.

How to Minimize Hallucinations   Some actions minimize the onset of hallucinations:

♦ Data Preprocessing: One of the first steps in reducing hallucinations is ensuring the training data is as clean and accurate as possible. This method can involve removing outliers or erroneous entries that could mislead the model.

♦ Model Fine-Tuning: After a model has been initially trained, it can be fine-tuned on a more specific, carefully curated dataset to avoid inaccuracies. This method can help the model become more reliable in generating accurate outputs.

♦ Output Verification: For critical applications, it is advisable to have a secondary system in place to verify the outputs generated by the LLM. This second system could be another, simpler model trained to flag potentially hallucinated content or even manual review by human experts.

♦ User Feedback: Allowing users to flag incorrect or nonsensical outputs in interactive applications can provide valuable data for further fine-tuning the model.

♦ Rate Limiting: In some cases, slowing down the rate at which the model generates output can allow more time for another system to assess the quality of the generated content, reducing the likelihood of hallucinations.

When used to generate recommendations around investing money or assets, large language models carry substantial risks of hallucinating content that seems plausible but leads actions astray. Without the reasoning capacity to deeply analyze causal relationships, LLMs may invent fictional data points, falsely identify trends based on made-up historical evidence, or make assertions that sound confident but have no factual basis.

While proper validation processes and combination with human expertise can help mitigate these risks, the underlying lack of grounded reasoning represents a gap we must account for when considering any high-stakes guidance generated by large language models today, especially in investing. In later chapters, we will explore how LLMs, despite their limitations, will help us create investment strategies.

Summary

We started our exploration by discussing how large language models like ChatGPT are poised to revolutionize quantitative analysis and algorithmic trading in finance. You learned about their potential to analyze earnings reports and regulatory filings, generate investment research notes, and even provide personalized stock recommendations tailored to an investor's goals and risk tolerance.

Next, we learned about natural language processing (NLP) and how it allows machines to understand human language. You learned about key NLP challenges like ambiguity and sarcasm detection. We covered critical NLP techniques like tokenization, named entity recognition to automatically extract key entities from text, machine translation, and text summarization. We also discussed valuable NLP applications in finance, like sentiment analysis of news and earnings calls.

After building an NLP foundation, you learned about the emergent capabilities of generative AI models to produce novel yet coherent outputs like images and text. We discussed the extensive learning phase, where these models ingest vast datasets to train statistical models that guide creative generation. You also learned about the different types of outputs these versatile models can produce from varying inputs.

Finally, we introduced large language models (LLMs) and transformers that take NLP and generative AI to the next level with immense numbers of parameters and context-understanding capabilities. However, you also learned about problems like biases and hallucinations in LLMs and ways to address them. To conclude, we set the stage for leveraging these advanced models to develop investment strategies in later chapters while accounting for their limitations.

This chapter explored large language models, a peak achievement in NLP and generative AI. LLMs like GPT-3 and GPT-4 represent the forefront of AI's capabilities to understand, interpret, and generate human language with a level of sophistication previously unimaginable. These models' potential to revolutionize industries, enhance decision-making, and even augment human creativity is immense. Yet, we must also solve the ethical and practical challenges they present. In essence, large language models exemplify the incredible potential of AI.

Coming Up Next

The next chapter explores some technical details of LLMs. It covers advanced topics, and you should read it only if you have a solid technical background and are interested in deploying these models. Otherwise, you can skip the chapter for now and jump straight to the ChatGPT chapter. You can return when you need an advanced understanding of LLMs for deploying specific applications.

In the next chapter, you will learn about the complex architectures like transformers and self-attention mechanisms that empower these models to understand nuance and context at an unprecedented level. We will unpack how enhancements like transfer learning and fine-tuning can optimize these models for specialized tasks and adjust key specifications like temperature and top-k tokens to control and improve output quality. We will also explore some of the latest state-of-the-art LLMs from organizations like Anthropic, Microsoft, Google, and Meta, pushing the boundaries of what is possible. Finally, we will discuss remaining challenges like computational demands and ethical considerations that responsibly guide ongoing innovation.

Check Your Understanding Questions

What is Natural Language Processing (NLP)?

◆ A. A field that focuses solely on speech recognition.
◆ B. A multidisciplinary field that helps machines understand, interpret, generate, and respond to human language.
◆ C. The process of translating languages automatically.

What are some critical challenges in Natural Language Processing (NLP)?

- ◆ A. Syntax and grammar checking.
- ◆ B. Ambiguity, context understanding, sarcasm, and sentiment detection.
- ◆ C. Only data storage and processing.

What is generative AI, and how does it differ from other AI forms?

- ◆ A. AI that solely focuses on analyzing data.
- ◆ B. AI designed to predict future trends based on past data.
- ◆ C. AI that focuses on creating new, original content based on learned patterns.

What makes large language models (LLMs) effective in NLP and generative AI?

- ◆ A. Their small and efficient structure.
- ◆ B. Their ability to generate human-like text and understand context thanks to training on vast datasets.
- ◆ C. They are faster than all other models.

What are "hallucinations" in the context of large language models?

- ◆ A. When the model makes errors due to overheating.
- ◆ B. When the model generates factually incorrect, nonsensical, or unsupported outputs.
- ◆ C. When the model predicts the future accurately.

How can biases in large language models impact their outputs?

- ◆ A. Biases have no real impact on model outputs.
- ◆ B. Biases can lead to the reinforcement of stereotypes and unfair decision-making.
- ◆ C. Biases make the models work faster.

What are some techniques used in NLP?

- ◆ A. Text summarization and machine translation.
- ◆ B. Only spell-checking.
- ◆ C. Only voice recognition.

Why is understanding the balance between novelty and coherence important in generative AI?

- ◆ A. It ensures that the generated content is original, but also understandable, and relevant.

- B. It is important only for aesthetic purposes.
- C. It helps in reducing the computational cost.

What role does continuous learning play in the effectiveness of LLMs?

- A. It has no significant role.
- B. It ensures that LLMs stay updated with the latest language trends and facts.
- C. It makes LLMs slower.

Why is addressing the issue of bias and hallucinations crucial in large language models?

- A. It ensures that LLMs continue to generate random outputs.
- B. It is crucial for maintaining AI systems' accuracy, reliability, and ethical responsibility.
- C. It is only necessary for legal compliance.

CHAPTER 4

Advanced Topics in LLMs

This chapter explores advanced topics in LLMs, and you need a solid technical background or to be interested in the deeper mechanics of training or fine-tuning these models for specialized tasks. It is designed as a comprehensive guide to understanding LLMs, whether for academic research, industry application, or personal project enhancement. You can safely go to the next chapter for now and return for reference when you need information related to an advanced project. The advanced LLM techniques covered here will become relevant when you are looking to squeeze out every drop of performance for demanding applications in investing.

Architectures Powering LLMs

LLMs stand at the forefront of AI's innovative edge, driving progress in fields as diverse as natural language processing, content generation, and semantic analysis. The efficacy and versatility of an LLM are significantly determined by its underlying architecture. This section unpacks the complex structures that power these sophisticated models, offering insights into their design, functionality, and the various approaches adopted in their development. By exploring these architectures' distinctive features, strengths, and limitations, you will understand what makes LLMs capable of their impressive feats and how to leverage these insights for specific computational tasks.

The architecture of an LLM plays a critical role in determining its performance for various tasks. Each architecture offers unique capabilities and limitations, from the simpler feed-forward neural networks to the revolutionary transformers. Understanding these architectures provides valuable insights into the inner workings of LLMs, aiding in selecting and developing models for specific applications.

Moreover, specialized architectures of large language models could enable customized solutions for financial analysis. Rather than retrofitting existing general-purpose LLMs, architectures could be designed from scratch with financial data and tasks in mind. These hypothetical specialized architectures may allow models to tune their entire computational focus on extracting signals and insights relevant to finance.

Financial LLMs based on customized architectures could specialize in time series forecasting, sentiment analysis, risk assessment, and other domain-specific capabilities. Their structures could be optimized for processing numeric data, quantitative signals, and evolving temporal dynamics rather than general language modeling.

Of course, developing such specialized financial LLMs involves significant research and innovation. However, the customizability and flexibility of neural networks provide ample room for financial customization in future LLM designs. The possibilities for tailoring these models to analyze statements, quantify market sentiment, forecast asset prices, optimize portfolios, and other critical financial tasks are abundant.

Considering this possibility, we will study the mechanisms that power modern large language models.

SELF-ATTENTION

Self-attention enables a model to assign varying importance to different input segments while analyzing a particular component. It allows the model to "pay attention" to portions of the input text, capturing the context and relationships between words or characters. This mechanism is crucial for understanding a sentence's semantics and generating coherent and contextually appropriate text.

In a typical LLM, the self-attention mechanism creates three vectors for each word in the input sequence: Query, Key, and Value. Specifically, the Query vector asks what parts of the input are relevant.

The Key vector contains context that helps determine relevance scores. Based on the scores, the Value vector holds the actual values to propagate through.

These Query, Key, and Value vectors compute attention scores between each word pair, determining how much focus or weight each word should receive. The scores are then used to aggregate the Value vectors, resulting in an output that captures the relevant contextual information for each word. By selectively focusing on pertinent context, self-attention enables capturing semantic meaning in language.

Why Self-Attention Matters:

- ◆ Contextual Understanding. Self-attention allows LLMs to understand the context in which a word appears, making it possible to disambiguate words with multiple meanings and generate contextually relevant text.
- ◆ Handling Long Sequences. Traditional recurrent neural networks (RNNs) and even some types of convolutional neural networks (CNNs) struggle with long sequences due to issues like vanishing or exploding gradients. Self-attention alleviates this by allowing direct connections between distant words.
- ◆ Parallelization. Unlike RNNs, where computations depend on the previous step, self-attention allows for parallelization as each word or token is processed simultaneously, leading to faster training times.

Self-attention is a cornerstone in state-of-the-art LLMs like GPT-3 and transformer-based architectures. These models can write coherent paragraphs, summarize text, answer questions, and generate code. The mechanism is so versatile that it's used in text-based models and models designed for image recognition and translation.

Self-attention has proven incredibly effective, albeit challenging. The computational cost can be high, especially for very long sequences. There's also ongoing research into making self-attention more interpretable, as the mechanism is often considered a "black box."

TRANSFORMERS

Transformers have revolutionized LLMs. Introduced in 2017, they discard the recurrent layers and focus on the Attention mechanism to draw global dependencies between input and output. This highly parallelizable architecture makes it incredibly efficient for handling large datasets. Transformers serve as the backbone for state-of-the-art models like GPT-3 and BERT.

Transformers come in various architectures: encoder-only, decoder-only, and encoder-decoder.

Encoder-Only Model

These models focus on generating a single output for each input token or sequence, making them well-suited for tasks like classification. They're bidirectional, incorporating a self-attention mechanism and a feed-forward neural network to process and understand input effectively. Consider a sentiment analysis task where a model determines if a press release is positive or negative. The encoder-only architecture processes each text part, understanding its overall sentiment, and then outputs a single prediction—positive or negative. Its bidirectional nature allows it to grasp the full context of the review, leading to a more accurate classification. Using self-attention, it attends to interactions between all words and phrases to truly understand the semantic meaning before outputting a positive or negative classification for the entire text.

A prominent example is BERT (Bidirectional Encoder Representations from Transformers). As an early transformer-based model, BERT processes input text using only a transformer encoder—hence the name "encoder-only." This architecture focuses on generating a contextualized representation of the entire input sequence rather than producing text token-by-token in a decoder. BERT's encoder-only approach allows for incorporating the full context of lengthy input sequences before making predictions.

Decoder-Only Model

Operating autoregressively, decoder-only models use each step's output as the input for the next step, functioning unidirectionally. They have uniquely learned to focus on the input sentence and the generated content so far, making them suitable for generative tasks like machine translation and text summarization without needing an encoder. An example is text generation, like creating a story. Starting with a prompt, the decoder-only model generates the story one piece at a time. Each new word or sentence segment is influenced by what has been generated so far, leading to a coherent and contextually relevant narrative. This unidirectional flow makes it adept at creating content that follows logically from the initial input. GPT3 is an example of a decoder-only model.

Encoder-Decoder Model

Originating from the original transformer model, this architecture involves encoding layers that process input and decoding layers that generate output sequences. Both encoder and decoder layers use a feed-forward neural network and an attention mechanism to enhance the model's understanding and output generation capabilities. A prime example is machine translation, like translating English to French. Here, the encoder processes the English sentence, understanding its context and meaning, and the decoder then generates the corresponding French sentence. Each part works in tandem, with the encoder providing a rich context for the decoder to produce accurate translations.

Improving LLMs

Building a large language model (LLM) involves significant investment, requiring extensive computational resources and vast datasets. However, the field's rapid evolution has introduced innovative strategies to enhance these models. Adjusting specifications, fine-tuning, and Transfer learning are at the forefront of these techniques, offering pathways to optimize LLMs' effectiveness and adaptability. We explore these strategies, elucidating how they make the most of the initial investment in creating and employing LLMs. Improving LLMs is easier using the concept of Transfer learning.

THE POWER OF TRANSFER LEARNING IN ARTIFICIAL INTELLIGENCE

Transfer learning is a revolutionary technique in AI that promotes a more efficient and practical approach to model training and deployment. By leveraging the knowledge gained from a previously trained model, this approach applies it to new but related problems. It's akin to human learning, where understanding one subject can enhance comprehension in another. In the context of LLMs, this means taking a model trained on a vast dataset and adapting it to perform specific tasks, conserving resources, enhancing model performance, and accelerating development.

LLMs like GPT-3 and BERT have dramatically benefited from Transfer learning. They leverage pre-trained models to perform various tasks without needing training from scratch. This adaptability has made LLMs highly versatile and powerful tools in multiple sectors.

Reasons why Transfer learning is pivotal for LLMs include:

◆ Resource Efficiency: Training LLMs from scratch is a resource-intensive process. Transfer learning mitigates this using pre-trained models, significantly reducing the computational power and data need.

◆ Improved Performance: LLMs, when fine-tuned, carry the extensive understanding from their initial broad training into specific tasks. This typically results in enhanced performance on these tasks compared to models trained only on task-specific data.

◆ Accelerated Development: By facilitating the reuse of existing models, Transfer learning speeds up LLMs' development and deployment cycle, enabling faster innovation and application across fields.

There are three types of Transfer learning in LLMs. These include:

1. Inductive Transfer Learning: This involves adapting a model trained on a general task (like language modeling) to a specific one (like text classification), leveraging its existing knowledge.

2. Transductive Transfer Learning: The model is adapted to new domains or languages, maintaining the task but altering the input space.

3. Unsupervised Transfer Learning: This technique adapts a model from one task to another without labeled data, using unsupervised methods to fine-tune the model on new types of content.

Real-World Applications and Challenges

Transfer learning has found applications in numerous areas, from healthcare, where it aids in diagnostics and patient care, to finance, where it's used to predict market trends and analyze documents.

It's also crucial in content creation and summarization. However, challenges still need to be addressed, such as ensuring the model doesn't carry over biases or irrelevant information (negative transfer) and identifying the most effective adaptation strategies.

FINE-TUNING LLMs

Fine-tuning is akin to giving an LLM a specialized training course, turning it from a generalist into a specialist. It involves adjusting a pre-trained model to specific data or tasks, enhancing its performance, and making it more relevant to particular applications.

The fine-tuning process involves training the LLM on a smaller, task-specific dataset, allowing it to adapt its existing knowledge to the new context. This specialized training makes the LLM more accurate and efficient in legal document analysis, medical diagnostics, or any other field-specific application.

While fine-tuning can significantly enhance an LLM's capabilities, it requires relevant, high-quality training data. There's also a need to balance specialization with the ability to perform various tasks to prevent the model from becoming too narrow in its application.

Adjusting Specifications in LLMs

LLMs' specifications refer to the adjustable parameters that significantly impact their behavior and outputs. Understanding the variables of LLMs is essential for harnessing their full potential. Whether you want to generate creative writing, concise answers, or anything in between, tweaking this specification can significantly impact the output. Therefore, it's crucial to understand what each variable does and how to use them effectively. This section will discuss the following variables: model size, tokenization, number of tokens, temperature, top-k and top-p, stop sequences, frequency, and presence penalties.

Model Size   The first specification variable to consider is the model size, essentially the number of parameters in the model. The model's size impacts the quality of the output. Larger models are generally more accurate and capable but come at the cost of computational speed and expense. They are often used for complex tasks like creative writing, while smaller models are more suitable for more straightforward tasks like classification.

Tokenization: The Building Blocks of Language for AI Imagine you're trying to assemble a jigsaw puzzle. The first step is to lay out all the individual pieces on the table. In LLMs like GPT-3 or GPT-4, tokenization serves a similar purpose. It breaks down text into shorter, manageable pieces, often called "tokens," so the model can understand and process it more easily. Let's explore tokenization and why it's crucial for these advanced AI systems.

In simple terms, tokenization is chopping a sentence into smaller parts, words, or smaller units, syllables, or individual letters. These smaller parts, tokens, are the model's building blocks for understanding the text. It is analogous to dividing a book into chapters; each chapter is part of the same book, but it's easier to handle and use in smaller portions.

By breaking down the text into tokens, tokenization makes it easier for the model to

- Understand Context: Tokens help the model grasp the meaning of each word in the context of the words around it.
- Identify Patterns: LLMs learn by recognizing patterns. Tokens make it easier to spot these patterns in language.
- Improve Accuracy: Smaller pieces are more straightforward to analyze, which helps the model make more accurate predictions and generate more relevant responses.

Tokenization might sound straightforward, but it has its complexities. For example, the word "New York" should ideally be one token, not two, because it represents a single entity. Similarly, contractions like "can't" could be broken down into "can" and "not" for better understanding. These nuances make tokenization a challenging yet fascinating part of language processing.

Tokenization is a foundational step in the functioning of LLMs. The process turns a text into manageable chunks, allowing the model to understand, analyze, and generate language. Just as you'd break down a complex task into smaller, more manageable tasks, tokenization breaks down complex sentences into smaller, more manageable pieces, setting the stage for these models' intricate work.

Number of Tokens This variable limits how many tokens (words or characters) the model will generate. This parameter allows you to control the length and detail of the generated text. A higher token limit will result in more detailed responses, whereas a lower limit will produce shorter, more concise text.

Temperature   Temperature is a crucial variable that controls the randomness in text generation. A higher temperature setting will make the model more creative but potentially less coherent. Conversely, a lower temperature will produce more cohesive and consistent text but may lack creativity. This variable is instrumental in balancing creativity and coherence in the generated text.

Top-k and Top-p   The top-k and top-p variables are other ways to control the output token. Top-k limits the next token to the top "k" most probable tokens, making the text more predictable but less diverse. Top-p is more dynamic and picks from the top tokens the sum of their probabilities, often used to exclude less probable outputs (Cohere 2022). Both of these parameters are useful for fine-tuning the diversity and accuracy of the generated text. For example, imagine you're using an AI to write a story. With top-k, if you set "k" to 5, the AI only considers the five most likely following words each time. This adjustment makes the story more predictable. With top-p, instead of a fixed number of words, it selects words that add up to a certain probability threshold, like 90 percent. This method sometimes includes more unusual word choices, making the story less predictable but potentially more creative. Both techniques help balance the randomness and coherence of the text the AI generates.

Stop Sequences, Frequency, and Presence Penalties   Stop Sequences act like a stop sign for AI models, telling them where to end the text, which helps control output length. Frequency and Presence Penalties reduce repetition: the former scales back on words that appear too often, while the latter does so regardless of how often a word appears. These tools are vital in making AI-generated text more diverse and less repetitive.

The Landscape of LLMs

LLMs are incredibly diverse, with each model offering unique capabilities and specializations. From search engine optimization to academic research and coding, these models revolutionize how we interact with technology. As they continue to evolve, the possibilities for their application seem endless.

Although this book is primarily about ChatGPT, it is helpful to mention that other similar models exist at the time of writing. The open-source models are especially relevant as they are easier to deploy and customize. Here are some of the most prominent (UC Today 2023).

BLOOM

Initiated by a co-founder of HuggingFace, this is a transformative large language model (LLM) in AI. It was collaboratively developed by BigScience's team, including Microsoft DeepSpeed, NVIDIA Megatron-LM, IDRIS/GENCI, PyTorch, and volunteers. Trained on approximately 366 billion tokens, BLOOM boasts 176 billion parameters and is proficient in 46 natural languages and 13 programming languages. This open-access, multilingual model is designed to democratize AI technology, providing public access to advanced language processing capabilities (BigScience 2023).

Claude

Developed by Anthropic (Anthropic 2023), a company founded by ex-OpenAI employees, Claude is a large language model known for its focus on safety, ethics, and efficiency. It's designed to be a helpful, harmless, and honest AI with carefully designed safety guardrails. Claude stands out for its ability to handle long inputs and is integrated into products like Notion AI and Quora's Poe. While it may be less capable than GPT-4, it excels in creative writing and answering open-ended questions, making it a strong contender in the AI chatbot space. Claude's unique approach to AI safety and its public benefit corporation status further distinguish it in the landscape of LLMs.

Cohere

Cohere (Cohere n.d.), a leading enterprise AI platform, offers powerful language models to build applications that understand and converse in text. Their models excel in search, meaning comprehension, and conversation, using advanced techniques like Retrieval Augmented Generation (RAG). Cohere's tools, including Coral for chatbots and knowledge assistants and Embed for semantic search, operate in English and more than 100 other languages. Their customizable models offer secure deployment options, making them versatile for various enterprise needs.

Falcon

Falcon 180B (Mukherjee n.d.), developed by the Technology Innovation Institute in the UAE, is a sizeable LLM. With 180 billion parameters and trained on 3.5 trillion tokens, Falcon 180B is a powerful open-source language model excelling in various NLP tasks. Its speed and multi-task language understanding capabilities stand out, ranking high on the Hugging Face leaderboard for pre-trained models. Falcon is particularly notable for its scalability, efficient use of computational resources, and impressive performance in multi-query attention for enhanced scalability.

LaMDA

LaMDA or Language Model for Dialogue Applications (Collins 2021), is a family of conversational large language models developed by Google. It was first introduced as Meena in 2020 and later evolved into LaMDA. This model is known for its ability to engage in open-ended conversations, trained on human dialogue and stories. It's designed to generate sensible, engaging, and context-specific responses, utilizing various symbolic text processing systems for enhanced accuracy. LaMDA represents a significant advancement in conversational AI, focusing on generating natural and engaging dialogues.

Llama

Created by Meta (formerly Facebook), Llama is a collection of large language models with varying sizes, varying from 7 to 65 billion parameters (Ivankov 2023). It is designed as a foundational model to support research in natural language processing and related AI subfields. Llama stands out for its training stability, fine-tuning capabilities, and ability to develop and implement other language models and specific NLP applications. Despite having fewer parameters and lower performance than models like GPT-4, Llama is more practical for widespread applications due to its open-source nature and lower computational costs. Llama 2 is the latest release of the model. It was trained in 40% more data than Llama 1, with double the context length.

Orca 2

Orca 2 is a language model developed by Microsoft with two versions having 7 billion and 13 billion parameters (Awadallah 2023). It surpasses models of similar size in performance and matches larger models up to 10 times its size. Orca 2 excels in reasoning tasks and zero-shot settings, demonstrating enhanced abilities typically found in much larger models. Its training involves fine-tuning Llama 2 base models on high-quality synthetic data, focusing on diverse reasoning techniques and optimal solutions for various tasks. Orca 2's success lies in its application of diverse reasoning techniques and identification of optimal solutions for different tasks, marking a significant step in diversifying language models' applications and deployment options.

PaLM 2

PaLM 2, Google's large language model, builds on the company's machine learning and responsible AI research. It excels in advanced reasoning, including coding, classification, and question answering, and boasts remarkable multilingual capabilities (Google n.d.). PaLM 2 integrates compute-optimal scaling, an improved dataset mixture, and architectural enhancements. It's rigorously evaluated for biases and potential harms and powers generative AI tools like the PaLM API and Bard, enhancing features in Google products like Gmail and Docs.

Gemini

Google's newest innovation, Gemini (Google Deepmind n.d), has been designed entirely for multimodal capabilities, allowing smooth integration and reasoning across various formats such as text, images, audio, video, and code. This groundbreaking model is the first to excel human experts in MMLU (Massive Multitask Language Understanding), a widely used measure for evaluating AI models' knowledge and problem-solving skills. Gemini has surpassed the current best-in-class performance in various text and coding benchmarks.

BERT

BERT or Bidirectional Encoder Representations from Transformers (Devlin and Chang 2018), developed by Google in 2018, represents a significant leap in NLP. Unlike previous models that processed words in a sentence sequentially, BERT understands each word's context to all other words in the sentence, thanks to its bidirectional approach. This deep understanding of sentence structure and meaning allows for more accurate and nuanced text interpretation. BERT's capabilities have been extensively use in various applications, such as improving search engine results, sentiment analysis, question-answering systems, and text classification. Its innovative architecture and training on massive datasets have made it a benchmark model in NLP, influencing subsequent developments in the field. BERT is an example of an encoder-only bidirectional model.

The landscape of LLMs of these technologies is as broad as it is profound. Each of these architectures has unique characteristics, strengths, and limitations, shaping the capabilities and applications of LLMs in various domains.

LLMs offer incredible opportunities, but they also come with challenges and responsibilities. The computational demands, ethical considerations, and potential biases inherent in these models necessitate ongoing research, thoughtful implementation, and critical evaluation.

Summary

By exploring the advanced topics in LLMs, we covered the critical architectures that empower these models to understand language and generate text. You learned how self-attention gives models contextual understanding by allowing them to focus on relevant words. We discussed transformers, which leverage self-attention for efficiently processing lengthy sequences. There are encoder-only models for classification tasks, decoder-only models for text generation, and encoder-decoder models ideal for translation.

We then explored methods for enhancing LLMs, as training these advanced models requires massive datasets and computing power. You learned about Transfer learning, which adapts a pre-trained model to new tasks, saving substantial resources. We also covered fine-tuning, which makes models better for particular applications through additional training on specific datasets. Additionally, we discussed how adjusting specifications like temperature and top-k in LLMs can balance creativity versus accuracy in their outputs.

Finally, we surveyed the landscape of prominent LLMs like BLOOM, Claude, and BERT, highlighting their unique capabilities and limitations. You learned how each contributes to the rich ecosystem of models moving AI forward. As these models grow more advanced, trends point toward making them more efficient, ethical, and versatile while integrating smoothly across diverse domains.

Coming Up Next

The next chapter will explore the specific case of ChatGPT in depth. We dissect its unique capabilities and address its limitations and the ethical landscape. The chapter also covers the prompt engineering and the future trajectory of ChatGPT and AI, underscoring their transformative potential across various sectors.

Check Your Understanding Questions

- ◆ Architectures of LLMs: What are the main neural network architectures discussed in the chapter, and how do they differ in handling sequential data?
- ◆ Self-Attention Mechanism: Explain the purpose of the self-attention mechanism in transformer models. How does it aid in understanding the context within sequences?
- ◆ Transformers and Their Variations: Describe the key differences between encoder-only, decoder-only, and encoder-decoder models in the context of transformers. Give an example of a task each type is best suited for.
- ◆ Transfer Learning: Define Transfer learning and explain its importance in LLMs. How does it benefit the process of model development and deployment?
- ◆ Fine-Tuning LLMs: What is fine-tuning, and why is it necessary to adapt large language models to specific tasks?
- ◆ Adjusting Specifications: List and explain at least three specification variables that can be adjusted in LLMs to influence their output. How might changing these variables affect the performance or output of an LLM?

- ◆ Model Comparisons: Compare and contrast two LLMs discussed in the chapter, focusing on their design, capabilities, and typical use cases.
- ◆ Challenges of LLMs: What are some main challenges associated with developing and deploying LLMs? Discuss computational, ethical, or bias-related challenges.
- ◆ Future of LLMs: Based on the chapter's content, what are the future directions or emerging trends in developing and applying LLMs?

PART II

ChatGPT and Stock Prediction

CHAPTER 5

What Is ChatGPT?

ChatGPT stands at the intersection of several advanced fields in artificial intelligence, primarily natural language processing (NLP), large language models (LLMs), and Generative AI. Each component is critical in enabling ChatGPT to understand and generate human-like text, making it an exceptional example of the capabilities of modern AI. In this chapter, we will explore ChatGPT's skills and limitations and learn how to obtain the best results using good prompting. In the next chapters, we will learn how to transform these abilities into investment insight.

ChatGPT is built upon the principles of NLP that allow ChatGPT not just to process the literal strings of text but also to understand the context and nuance in a conversation, much like a human would. LLMs, the engines driving ChatGPT, are trained on extensive amounts of text data, enabling them to comprehend and generate language. ChatGPT's advanced natural language processing skills allow it to understand various types of textual data spanning industry reports, financial statements, earnings call transcripts, investment theses, and more.

Learning from diverse sources, encompassing various styles, topics, and language structures, allows ChatGPT to create responses that are contextually appropriate and rich in content, mirroring the depth and versatility of human language. Unlike traditional AI models that only analyze or classify data, Generative AI enables ChatGPT to produce original content.

Whether writing in different styles, answering questions, or even creating entirely new concepts, ChatGPT uses its generative capabilities to go beyond mere language replication, venturing into creativity and innovation. Creating scenarios will be very useful when using ChatGPT in an investing context. For instance, ChatGPT can generate insightful "what-if" stories of how demand shifts, input costs, and supply bottlenecks may strain profitability when investigating if a firm has the resilience to navigate an impending recession.

Together, these components make ChatGPT a sophisticated tool, not just for mimicking human conversation but for providing insights, solutions, and even creative content, showcasing the vast potential of AI in our daily interactions and tasks.

ChatGPT uses the GPT (Generative Pre-trained Transformer) architecture, fine-tuned explicitly for conversational contexts and instruction following. It was developed by OpenAI to understand and generate human-like text in an everyday context. It has been designed to interact with us coherently and provide contextually relevant and surprisingly human-like answers.

The model has potential applications in various sectors, from customer service automation to mental health counseling. Its ability to understand and generate text closely mimicking human language has made it a subject of awe and scrutiny. Understanding the capabilities and limitations of models like ChatGPT becomes crucial as we increasingly integrate artificial intelligence into decision-making.

Capabilities

The capabilities of ChatGPT arise from its robust training methodology, which combines a broad understanding of language with specialized fine-tuning. These skills can be categorized into key areas.

ENGAGING IN HUMAN-LIKE CONVERSATIONS

ChatGPT can understand our requests and generate contextually relevant, coherent responses. It can simulate a wide range of conversational styles depending on our input and the intended tone of the conversation. In finance, there are multiple potential applications. For example, the model can take complex financial data and describe the key takeaways in clear, understandable language.

FOLLOWING INSTRUCTIONS

ChatGPT's ability to understand and follow complex instructions makes it versatile for various tasks. The model can recognize our intent and generate appropriate responses, whether it is a request to draft an email, explain a concept, or even create computer code.

There are many potential applications relating to investing. Whether analyzing investments, generating reports, assessing risk, or ensuring compliance, ChatGPT can adaptively follow specifications to handle requests with unique parameters and objectives. This versatility to produce tailored output makes it well-suited for the highly variable requirements of using it in an investment context.

RUNNING CODE

ChatGPT can write computer code very well. Moreover, it can execute code written in the Python programming language. Python is a popular and user-friendly coding language for all types of applications, including data analysis and machine learning. ChatGPT features an integrated Python environment, which means it can run Python code directly within its system. This allows it to demonstrate coding examples and solutions by showing the live output.

For instance, ChatGPT can write and execute a Python script that performs a financial calculation, analyzes a dataset, or automates a task. Viewing the code output helps further understanding and problem solving. While code execution expands ChatGPT's capabilities, you do not need programming knowledge to benefit. The system can handle writing, explaining, and running code on your behalf.

Notably, the ability to run code also increases ChatGPT's overall reasoning capabilities. By executing code, ChatGPT can demonstrate concepts in action, test hypotheses, and validate its responses and recommendations. Whether it is showing financial analysis through a coded simulation, building intuition on a mathematical theorem by scripting calculations, or checking its textual explanations by running associated code, the hands-on execution strengthens ChatGPT's abilities. It allows the system to connect abstract reasoning to tangible outputs. ChatGPT's integrated coding environment fundamentally expands what it can infer and explain.

REAL-TIME WEB BROWSING

ChatGPT has real-time web browsing capabilities, allowing it to access and retrieve up-to-date information online. ChatGPT can look up recent news, gather current data, and read from websites. Rather than being confined to a static dataset, ChatGPT can leverage the internet to look up recent news, collect the latest financial data, analyze current market trends, study emerging technologies, and consume up-to-the-minute content from authoritative websites.

LANGUAGE UNDERSTANDING

ChatGPT can understand and generate human language. This understanding is not limited to the syntax and grammar rules but extends to the semantics and context. The model can comprehend nuances in speech, such as idioms, metaphors, and cultural references.

This skill allows ChatGPT to accurately interpret the subtleties within corporate communications, research reports, regulatory edicts, earnings call statements, and other complex documents that shape investment research. Identifying nuance helps us make informed decisions—whether reading between the lines of cautious executive guidance or understanding the implications of delicate central bank phrasing.

CONTEXT AWARENESS

ChatGPT can maintain context within a conversation. Unlike simpler chatbots that treat each input as an isolated query, ChatGPT can remember previous exchanges within the same conversation. This context awareness allows the model to provide more coherent and relevant responses, enhancing the conversational experience.

This continuity offers tangible benefits for investments. For instance, we might first ask ChatGPT to assess a report about the market landscape for electric vehicles. The model would assimilate these industry reports and data. We could then ask to narrow the focus to a specific electric car firm for consideration. Thanks to its context awareness, ChatGPT could directly apply inferences about the overall market to the specified stock, offering tailored insights.

Similarly, ChatGPT could maintain contextual frameworks while generating models that involve multiple interdependent variables adjusted across iterations—invaluable for scenario planning. Its memory streamlines workflows that demand a consistent viewpoint, bolstering productivity. By preserving context, ChatGPT delivers flows of analysis that mirror human reasoning.

SPECIALIZED KNOWLEDGE

Thanks to the extensive pre-training phase, ChatGPT has a broad general knowledge base that spans various domains, from science and technology to history and pop culture. While not a substitute for expert advice, the model can provide informative and fact-based answers to various questions.

While not an expert, ChatGPT's extensive training equips it with literate financial and economic knowledge. This means it can fluently discuss concepts that shape investment analysis, even if it cannot match the sophistication of specialized forecasting. For example, the model can articulate how inflation dynamics, like supply-side shocks and shifting consumer demand, influence the economy. It can explain how indicators like unemployment and GDP growth factor into monetary policy and market expectations. ChatGPT can connect socioeconomic trends to stock and sector rotations, such as aging demographics driving healthcare spending.

CREATIVITY AND FLEXIBILITY

ChatGPT is not just a question-answering machine; it is also capable of creative tasks like writing, brainstorming ideas, and even generating new algorithms using its coding skills. The model can synthesize disparate information, recognize obscured patterns, and make original connections that humans may overlook.

Its flexibility allows it to adapt to different conversational styles and tones, whether you are looking for a formal business report or a casual chat about movies. ChatGPT has the flexibility to communicate insights effectively to different investor types. It can generate detailed research reports for institutional investors or simplified stock explanations for retail traders according to their needs.

REAL-TIME ADAPTABILITY

ChatGPT can adapt to the conversation in real time, adjusting its responses based on our inputs. This adaptability makes it suitable for dynamic tasks that require back-and-forth interaction, such as troubleshooting, role-playing scenarios, or collaborative writing.

When developing an investment thesis, having a partner to bounce ideas off can reveal new angles. ChatGPT can assume that agile role thanks to its real-time adaptability. As we raise rough ideas or hypotheses about a potential stock, sector, or strategy, ChatGPT can reinforce credible notions, elaborate on gaps, and reshape flawed logic.

ChatGPT's flexibility allows us to externalize our thoughts and sharpen them collaboratively. Whether playing devil's advocate to stress test a shaky principle you propose or exploring your sudden epiphany to uncover validity, it is an agile idea refiner optimized for speculative dynamism innate to investing conjecture. The system becomes an on-demand, ever-adjusting sounding board for your investing ideation.

ETHICAL AND SAFE INTERACTIONS

Through fine-tuning, ChatGPT is trained to adhere to ethical guidelines and avoid generating harmful or inappropriate content. While imperfect, this capability ensures safer and more responsible interactions.

MULTILINGUAL SUPPORT

Although primarily trained on English data, ChatGPT has some capacity to understand and generate text in multiple languages. This feature broadens its applicability to a global audience, although the proficiency can vary depending on the language.

ChatGPT's impressive abilities in many domains make it suitable for various tasks. Moreover, these capabilities evolve thanks to ongoing training and feedback, making ChatGPT one of the most advanced large language models available.

FINE-TUNING FOR CUSTOMIZATION

Some versions of ChatGPT allow for fine-tuning to specific tasks or domains. ChatGPT's base capabilities can be enhanced through additional training on specialized financial datasets like corporate statements, trading records, loan histories, insurance claims, and personal finance documents.

For example, ingesting historical trading data can optimize ChatGPT's ability to develop profitable algorithmic investing strategies. Exposure to loan default and consumer credit records allows more accurate credit risk analysis when underwriting new borrowers or modeling losses. The supplemental training on relevant financial texts can sharpen ChatGPT's reasoning and recommendations to augment human expertise in assessing risk, constructing portfolios, maximizing wealth, and navigating uncertain economic environments. This fine-tuning process makes ChatGPT adaptable and customizable to various needs and applications.

Limitations

While ChatGPT is a powerful conversational agent with a wide range of capabilities, we must recognize its limitations. Understanding these constraints not only helps in setting realistic expectations but also guides future improvements. Here are some of the fundamental limitations:

LACK OF DEEP UNDERSTANDING

ChatGPT can generate coherent and contextually relevant text, but it does not truly understand the content it generates. It lacks a complete world model, meaning it does not have a full conceptual representation of how the world's interconnected systems, events, and incentives shape outcomes. As a result, ChatGPT struggles to understand the effects of complex causal forces. It can sometimes output nonsensical or factually incorrect answers that might sound plausible but are not grounded. This issue arises specifically when the tasks need many reasoning steps. While ChatGPT can successfully link a couple of steps (sometimes by just asking it to think step by step), tasks that require extensive reasoning are out of reach. Breaking the tasks into many small steps and ensuring the model does not rely too much on its output can help.

For example, outcomes like asset prices, regulator decisions, firm actions, and consumer behaviors depend on many factors, including political catalysts, social trends, market psychology, corporate governance, and macroeconomic environments. ChatGPT cannot fully comprehend the relationships between the entire set of variables. While it can discuss concepts and events, it misses the complete picture that connects the dots at a fundamental level. Therefore, asking ChatGPT to reliably predict, evaluate, or explain scenarios that depend on multilayered context goes beyond its capabilities.

While seemingly logical, its outputs are not grounded in the comprehensive reasoning required to capture this complexity. To be fair, this task is also challenging for humans.

While ChatGPT can discuss financial topics and even offer reasonable-sounding commentary, its level of comprehension has clear limitations. Without a genuine grasp of market principles, asset valuation techniques, portfolio construction theory, and other specialized knowledge, ChatGPT often oversimplifies complex concepts or misses nuances that shape real-world trading and risk decisions.

For instance, ChatGPT might highlight superficially relevant metrics when analyzing a company without considering important qualitative aspects or industry-specific contexts that impact fundamental value. Its descriptions may also fail to capture the depth of factors that underlie managerial choices. While articulate, the insights may risk incompleteness.

Additionally, lacking an integrated world model means ChatGPT does not have an anchoring set of fundamental principles to ground its assessments. As a result, its evaluations and forecasts around complex scenarios risk inconsistency. For example, when estimating the market impact of an event, two similar but slightly different queries could result in entirely different speculative projections that downplay or overemphasize some investment consequences. ChatGPT cannot maintain a steady analytical logic without a robust world model. This is a smaller issue for simple tasks, so following the previous advice of using the model for small tasks will help.

SHORT-TERM MEMORY

The architecture of ChatGPT has a limited "memory" in terms of the number of words (tokens) it can consider in one go. This limitation affects its ability to maintain context in extended conversations or understand queries requiring recalling several previous interactions. The latest models have context windows of around 32,000 tokens, so this limitation primarily applies to long documents.

ChatGPT's constrained short-term memory poses challenges for producing lengthy and structurally coherent reports. When asked to compile an investment research report, ChatGPT may lose the narrative thread across sections, repeating points or losing connective logic. If the report attempts to link insights across a series of interviewed experts, ChatGPT may forget prior viewpoints and fail to synthesize perspectives. Tables, charts, and paragraphs inserted may lack tight integration with the surrounding commentary. Or worse, with a loose memory grasp, ChatGPT may contradict itself on market assumptions and conclusions at different places within the same document. Without an integrated framework persisting in working memory, output cohesion suffers, undermining document quality and readable flow.

A technique that helps with this issue is a top-down approach. This method involves first asking for an outline of the topics covered in the document. Then, the model will fill this outline with specific ideas for each topic. Finally, the model can start writing each section. However, it is necessary to confirm the consistency of the outputs manually or with a different instance of an LLM.

ChatGPT's limited short-term memory also hinders its processing of extremely lengthy content like legal contracts, research publications, or regulatory filings. For example, ChatGPT can only retain and connect so much context at once when asked to digest and concisely summarize a corporate annual report. As a result, its summaries may fail to capture key details buried in the documents or lose sight of overarching themes that tie disparate sections together. Subtleties in the source material can be glossed over. Or worse, ChatGPT may fixate on and repeat superficially attention-grabbing details while omitting more fundamental concepts that require grasping the full scope. Without the capacity to internalize all salient points, its summaries risk cherry-picking pieces or distorting emphasis improperly. So, while helpful for distilling moderate content, highly concise summaries of vast publications tend to be subpar.

To work around this limitation, a bottom-up approach is helpful. This approach consists of passing a short amount of text at a time and asking ChatGPT to outline the main ideas and findings. Once done with all the text, there can be a second summarization of the main ideas and findings to produce a final report. This approach also has the advantage of being easier to audit.

SENSITIVITY TO INPUT PHRASING

The model's performance can vary depending on how a question or prompt is phrased. A slight rewording can yield a more accurate or helpful response, which can be challenging in applications requiring consistent reliability. It is best to assign tasks with unambiguous interpretations. For example, instead of asking about the prospects of a specific stock based on some news, asking whether its stock price is likely to go up is preferred. Moreover, it is helpful to run a manual assessment of how different prompts affect the outcome by testing interactively with some actual data. Furthermore, this problem is minor if the task is simple, so manually breaking the task into small pieces that can then be fed to ChatGPT is helpful.

ETHICAL AND SAFETY CONCERNS

Despite efforts to make the model adhere to ethical guidelines, ChatGPT can sometimes generate politically biased, offensive, or otherwise inappropriate content. While there are safety mitigations in place, they are not foolproof.

COMPUTATIONAL COSTS

Running large language models like ChatGPT requires significant computational resources, which can limit widespread deployment, especially in resource-constrained environments. Carefully setting up a smaller experiment before deployment may save some costs.

DATA PRIVACY

Data privacy is always a concern since the model is trained on a large amount of text data. The model is designed not to remember personal information, but the potential for misuse exists, especially if the model is deployed in applications that handle sensitive information.

MULTILINGUAL LIMITATIONS

Although ChatGPT has multilingual capabilities, its proficiency is highest in English. The quality of understanding and generation can be inconsistent for other languages, affecting their usability for a global audience.

DEPENDENCE ON TRAINING DATA

The model's knowledge was frozen during its last training session, meaning it does not update its information in real time. The web browsing capabilities help to a certain extent, although the model needs to be told explicitly to browse, and it may click on irrelevant links.

This limitation impacts its use when asking for investment recommendations since it does not have the latest information available. To address this issue, it is best to provide the specific context needed directly, instead of asking the model to browse. For example, we can provide a press release rather than ask the model about it without context.

INABILITY TO LEARN DURING INTERACTION

ChatGPT cannot learn or adapt its behavior over time based on specific interactions. Each conversation is stateless, meaning the model does not learn from past conversations to improve future interactions. This means that when a new instance is created, it will not retain the information from other queries. In investing, this limitation implies that the model cannot use the information from other firms when asking about a new one if each firm is treated separately.

HALLUCINATIONS

ChatGPT and other LLMs tend to "hallucinate" information or present confidently stated falsehoods. This happens when the model generates answers that seem plausible and logical but are incorrect or nonsensical. Hallucinations can be particularly challenging to detect because the model writes responses with a tone of authority and conviction, making the false information seem credible. This limitation requires us to verify information from ChatGPT, especially when using it for important decisions or understanding complex topics.

For example, ChatGPT may confidently provide false investment statistics, distorted risk assessments, and imaginary historical patterns that seem credible but lack factual verification. For instance, when asked for the largest historical single-day gain for the S&P 500, ChatGPT could cite a fictional 15% surge. Or it may hallucinate an investment strategy backtest showing stable 30% annual returns that never occurred.

Problematically, these convincing-sounding falsehoods often align logically with the prompts provided. And ChatGPT can weave elegant narratives explaining why its delusions represent reality. Yet without checking external references, we risk acting on manufactured financial data points and reasoning with no authentic basis.

The potential consequences span from simple embarrassment when relaying imaginary indices to clients to catastrophic portfolio losses if executing trades based on ChatGPT's market hallucinations instead of truth. No investment model or human can perfectly predict the future, but grounding analysis in objective data history limits imaginative risks. Blending ChatGPT's reasoning with ongoing verification thus remains key to balancing productivity with practicality when investing.

To reduce hallucinations in investment guidance, we should decompose broad queries into small parts to simplify ChatGPT's role. Additionally, offering specific contextual reference points helps ground ChatGPT's responses in reality rather than pure imagination. For example, providing an excerpt from a company's annual report may help. We should split complex information requests into limited pieces and provide reference data whenever possible.

Understanding these limitations helps make the most out of ChatGPT while being aware of its constraints. These areas require further research and development to make conversational AI more robust, reliable, and safe. In the meantime, with a thoughtful formulation of prompts as a guide, we can strategically channel ChatGPT's strengths and avoid problematic responses.

What Is a Prompt?

A prompt is an initial text or input—a question, statement, or command—we give to the model to elicit a response. Our part of the conversation guides the AI's subsequent output. For example, a prompt can be "explain machine learning" or "design a website about data science."

Prompts unlock ChatGPT's capabilities. The effectiveness and relevance of ChatGPT's outputs are primarily influenced by how a prompt is structured, making understanding and crafting effective prompts crucial for harnessing the full potential of ChatGPT.

Your prompt could be a question, a statement, or even a request for a story or explanation. It sets the tone and the topic for what comes next.

PROMPT TYPES

Prompts are essential for interacting with language models. They provide context and direction. Without a prompt, a model would not have a reference point or know how to generate a relevant response. Prompts guide the model's vast knowledge and capabilities and help us harness the model's power in specific and directed ways. There are multiple ways to classify prompts:

Open-Ended vs. Closed-Ended Prompts

◆ Open-ended prompts allow for a wide range of responses. They do not have a specific or singular answer. For instance, "Tell me about the Renaissance" is open-ended because the model could approach the topic from various angles, discussing art, history, key figures, and more.

◆ Closed-ended prompts, on the other hand, typically have a specific answer. Questions like "What is the capital of Japan?" or "Is water H2O?" are closed-ended because they expect a definite and concise response. These prompts are easy to check for hallucinations since there is usually a correct answer.

Information-Seeking vs. Creative Prompts

◆ Information-seeking prompts are designed to extract factual, detailed, or specific information from the model. They are often direct and to the point, such as "Explain the process of photosynthesis" or "List the benefits of exercise."

◆ Creative prompts aim to harness the model's ability to generate imaginative, original, or artistic content. "Write a short story about a robot investing" or "Describe a world where the sky is green on Tuesdays."

◆ We must match the prompt category with the desired outcome to get the most relevant and helpful results from the model.

PROMPT ENGINEERING

Prompt engineering is the art of designing helpful prompts to guide ChatGPT in generating the most valuable and accurate responses. Our prompts drive the answers ChatGPT produces.

While OpenAI tries to make simple prompts give relevant answers and prompt engineering irrelevant, there are still significant differences in the type of answers we get when trying different styles. In some sense, it is a feature, not a bug, that ChatGPT complies with our instructions.

Through prompts, we unlock the varied capabilities of ChatGPT, whether you are looking for a detailed explanation of a complex concept, a creative story, or help to understand a mathematical problem. Prompts help output the exact tale or information we want.

Prompt Engineering General Guidelines

Information Retrieval   Framing a prompt becomes crucial when trying to extract factual, detailed, and accurate information. Following these steps helps to craft prompts for information retrieval:

1. Direct Questions: Start with a straightforward question like "What is the capital of France?" or "Explain the process of photosynthesis."
2. Specify the Format: If you are looking for information in a particular format, mention it in the prompt. For instance, "List the main causes of World War I in bullet points."
3. Avoid Leading Language: Avoid using leading or loaded terms to ensure unbiased information. Instead of "Why is solar energy the best renewable source?" ask, "What are the advantages of solar energy compared to other renewable sources?"
4. Request Sources: If you want the model to cite sources or provide references, include that in the prompt, like "Provide a summary of quantum mechanics and search online for relevant sources." ChatGPT can currently search online for information, albeit its capability is limited.
5. Fact Check: Any answer from ChatGPT can be hallucinated and sound correct but be entirely made up. Sources are especially prone to hallucinations. Always verify the responses. An imperfect solution involves asking ChatGPT or other LLM in separate conversations to check the answers for accuracy. This method will decrease the likelihood of falsehood, but manually fact-checking responses used in critical applications is imperative.

Creative Writing   Prompts for creative writing aim to spark imagination and generate unique content. Here is how to frame them:

1. Open-ended Starters: Begin with an open-ended statement or question like "Imagine a world where . . ." or "Describe a day in the life of a dragon."

2. Provide Themes or Constraints: Giving a theme or setting constraints can guide the creative process. For example, "Write a short story set in a post-apocalyptic world."

3. Use Inspirational Quotes or Images: Sometimes, a quote or an image description can be a creative prompt. "Write a poem inspired by the quote: 'Not all those who wander are lost.'"

4. Be Specific: Complex prompts with specific requests are more likely to obtain original answers. For example, the prompt "Give me a story about a dragon" will likely result in a worse outcome than "Give me a puzzling short story about a Norwegian dragon being hunted by early humans. This dragon is injured and attacks humans out of fear when they come nearby. Add a plot twist. Set it in an ice age."

Providing detailed prompts to ChatGPT enhances the model's ability to generate accurate and relevant responses. The more specific your prompt, the less guessing the model has to do, leading to more precise outcomes.

Include Details More specific details and constraints in your prompts can help the model generate higher-quality responses. We reduce guesswork and opportunities for factual errors or tangents by narrowing the focus. Some tips:
Examples:

◆ Vague: "Tell me about space."
◆ Detailed: "Explain the star formation process in the Orion Nebula."

Use Delimiters Delimiters like dashes, bullet points, or clear headings help ChatGPT distinguish different parts of your prompt, enabling more structured and coherent responses. Examples include:

◆ Without Delimiters: "Write a story about a pirate treasure map discovery followed by a surprising twist."
◆ With Delimiters: "Story Request: 1. Setting—a deserted island; 2. Main plot—the discovery of a pirate treasure map; 3. Twist—the treasure is actually a time capsule from the future."

Provide Reference Text A reference text can be constructive when seeking information or analyzing a particular subject. If the text is lengthy, we can ask ChatGPT to summarize each part and request a summary of the final result. Examples:

◆ Direct Reference: "Based on this abstract and introduction [text goes here], can you summarize the key findings about renewable energy advancements?"
◆ Summarization Steps: "I have a long article about the history of the internet. I will provide excerpts from each section. Please summarize each part first, and then give an overall summary."

Common Issues and How to Avoid Them

There are some common issues related to prompts that we might encounter. Recognizing and avoiding these issues can significantly enhance the quality of the model's outputs.

Ambiguity

◆ Problem: Ambiguous prompts can lead to vague or off-target responses. The model might not provide the desired answer if a prompt is unclear or isn't specific enough.
◆ How to Avoid: Be as straightforward as possible in your prompts. If seeking factual information, phrase your prompt in a way that narrows down the context. Example: Instead of making the request, "Tell me about apples," we could ask, "What are the nutritional benefits of eating apples?" Always fact check.

Overcomplication

◆ Problem: Overly complex prompts can confuse the model or lead to unnecessarily lengthy responses. ChatGPT has limited reasoning capabilities and cannot correctly manage tasks requiring multi-step reasoning.
◆ How to Avoid:
  • Keep prompts short and ask for only the information you are interested in. Example: Instead of asking, "What are the benefits and drawbacks associated with caffeinated beverages?" ask, "What are five pros and cons of drinking caffeinated drinks? No explanation."
  • Break the task into manageable chunks. Instead of using the prompt, "Here is a document [long document]. Help me

correct the grammar and improve it," use, "Here is part of a document [short section of the long document]. Help me correct the grammar and improve it."

Ethical Considerations   Problem: Some prompts can lead to ethically questionable, biased, or potentially harmful outputs. While ChatGPT will usually refuse to answer with dangerous or illegal information, subtle biases may arise in the answers.

How to Avoid:

♦ Be aware of the likely biases in the model and craft prompts that mitigate them.
♦ Avoid prompts that might lead to harmful or misleading results if used. For example, "Here is a chemical component [component]. What happens if I add nitrogen to the mix?" ChatGPT may hallucinate the final compound even if it gets some steps correct.
♦ Review and verify the output, primarily if the model is used for sensitive topics.

There is recent work trying to systematize the process of prompt creation. The Prompt Engineering Canvas is a framework that simplifies designing effective prompts. (López 2023)

THE PROMPT ENGINEERING CANVAS

The Prompt Engineering Canvas is a structured framework designed to help you craft effective prompts for AI models. It simplifies the process of prompt creation by breaking it down into manageable components, ensuring that every aspect of the interaction is considered. The canvas acts as a blueprint, helping us visualize and plan our prompts, making the interaction with AI models more predictable and aligned with our goals.

Key Components of the Canvas

Central to the Prompt Engineering Canvas are its nine integral components, each designed to shape and refine the AI interaction:

Goal	Persona	Task
How	Audience	Output
Constraints	Models	Quality assurance

The Prompt Engineering Canvas helps you communicate your intentions to ChatGPT without ambiguity. By ensuring that AI-generated responses are accurate and aligned with your objectives, this canvas serves as a roadmap to success in AI interactions. Whether crafting prompts for content generation, problem solving, or creative endeavors, the canvas offers a structured approach, revolutionizing AI communication.

Each component of the Prompt Engineering Canvas plays a pivotal role in crafting effective AI prompts.

Goal: Problem or Purpose   It is crucial to clearly define the overall goal or specific problem we intend to solve with ChatGPT. This step lays the foundation for your interaction, aligning the AI capabilities with your end goal. The objective is sometimes different from the task, as sometimes it is convenient to split an objective into several parts. For example, for the "Develop a marketing strategy" objective, the first task might be "Brainstorm campaign ideas."

Examples of goals:

- ◆ Write a book about travel
- ◆ Learn a programming language
- ◆ Develop a marketing strategy
- ◆ Improve personal productivity
- ◆ Explore travel options
- ◆ Learn to cook

It goes in the prompt as "My goal is . . ."

Persona & Style   In "Persona & Style," we specify the role or identity we want ChatGPT to adopt and the communication style. Depending on your objectives, this identity can range from formal to technical to casual and creative.

Examples of Persona include:

- A supportive coach for motivational messages

- A technical expert for detailed scientific explanations

- A creative writer for crafting engaging stories

- A friendly advisor for personal development tips

- A professional consultant for business strategy advice

- A famous person, for example, Leonardo da Vinci

- A tech tool (e.g., the command line of Linux)

The way to put it is "Act as if you were . . ." or "Assume you are an expert in . . ."

Examples of styles:

♦ Formal or Informal
♦ Authoritative, Informative, Casual, Trustworthy, Straightforward
♦ Empathic or Friendly
♦ Confrontational
♦ Inspirational
♦ Urgent or Persuasive
♦ Poetic, Narrative, Shakespearian

The way to put it in the prompt is "Use a . . . style"

Task Definition: The What   The "Task Definition" outlines the specific action or content we need from ChatGPT. This clarity ensures that the AI understands what you are asking it to do.

Examples of tasks might be:

♦ "Help me create an outline for my book."
♦ "Explain to me what Python is."
♦ "Brainstorm ideas for a campaign."
♦ "Generate a list of healthy recipes."
♦ "Explain to me the basics of quantum physics."
♦ "Create a short fiction story set in medieval times."
♦ "Provide a step by step guide to meditation."
♦ "Provide a summary of the latest research on AI2."
♦ "Write an article/essay/social media post/blog posting."
♦ "Write a cover letter for . . ."
♦ "Generate SEO words for my campaign."
♦ "Correct my text."
♦ "Correct errors in my code."
♦ "Explain how to cook grilled fish."

The way to put it in the prompt is "Your task is to . . ."

The How   In this component, we define the approach ChatGPT should use for the task, guiding how the AI approaches it and ensuring it aligns with your intent and style preferences.

The way to express this at the prompt is "For this task, you should . . ." or "You should do . . .".

Some examples might be:

- "Do it step-by-step."
- "After each section, ask me if I want to continue."
- "Take these examples as a basis (and then provide examples)."

Audience Context: The Whom   Audience context requires us to consider the intended audience of the ChatGPT response. Tailoring content to the audience ensures relevance and impact.

Considerations may include:

- Age group (e.g., children, adults)
- Knowledge level (e.g., beginners, experts)
- Cultural background
- Specific interests or needs

The way to express this in the prompt is "The audience for this task is . . ."

Output Format: Crafting the Output   "Output Format" is used to select the desired format for the ChatGPT response. For example, it can be text, tables, code snippets, or poems.

Possible formats include:

- A well-structured essay
- A series of vignettes
- A fictional narrative
- A formatted code fragment
- An infographic or visual representation
- A table or list
- Code (e.g., Python code)
- Plain text, markdown, or rich text
- HTML
- A Gantt chart

The way to put it in the prompt is "Output must be in the form of . . ."

Constraints & Assumptions   Here, we define the constraints or assumptions that guide ChatGPT responses. These include word limits, terminology preferences, or sensitivity to specific subjects.

Examples of restrictions:

◆ "Limit responses to 100 words."
◆ "Avoid technical jargon for a general audience."
◆ "Focus on green solutions."
◆ "Stick to a specific narrative style."
◆ "Exclude certain controversial subjects."
◆ "Avoid sensitive subjects."

The way to put it in the prompt is "For this task, consider the following constraint(s) . . ."

Models, Frameworks, and Techniques: Which Tools to Use?   Suggesting specific models, frameworks, or techniques for ChatGPT to consider can improve the quality and relevance of your responses.

For example:

◆ "Use Bono's Six Hats technique to analyze this project."
◆ "Use the Brainstorming technique."
◆ "Run Python code to . . ."
◆ "Use Porter's Five Forces to analyze my business idea."
◆ "Apply the Lean Canvas Model to show what my business idea should look like."
◆ "Use instructional design best practices for this course."

The way to put it in the prompt is "Use . . . model/technique/ framework for this task."

Quality Assurance: Ensuring Excellence   Finally, "quality assurance" consists of establishing the quality standards of the response. This part ensures that the outcome meets your expectations and requirements.

Quality criteria can be:

- Accuracy of information
- Creativity and originality
- Relevance to the task
- Clarity and understandability
- Appropriateness to the specified constraints and style.

Examples:

- "Review each of your responses and ensure they meet the requirements and are consistent with each other."
- "Make sure you haven't missed anything in previous steps."

Putting It All Together: An Engineered Prompt   Here is an example of a draft prompt made using the Prompt Engineering Canvas:

- My goal is: To learn about stock markets
- Assume you are: A stock market expert
- Your task is to: Write an outline of a stock market course
- To do the task, you have to consider: Use a step-by-step approach
- The audience is: A person with basic knowledge about stock markets
- The output format is: Plain text
- Consider the following constraints and assumptions: The course duration is two weeks maximum
- Use the following tools: Best instructional design practices
- To assure quality, you have to: Validate the most important knowledge to be included in the course

Provide this information to ChatGPT using the following instructions:

Your objective is to refine a draft prompt provided by the user. Your task is to optimize the prompt for clarity, completeness, and effectiveness, ensuring that it is perfectly understandable by ChatGPT. If the draft prompt lacks essential information, your *role is to fill in the gaps appropriately. The final output should be a single paragraph, and formatted in plain text. The audience for the enhanced prompt is ChatGPT itself, so the language should be tailored to what the model can understand best. Please adhere strictly to these guidelines to ensure the highest quality output. Do not answer the question directly. Your task is to generate a prompt that ChatGPT can use to answer the question. Think step by step. The draft prompt will be enclosed within angle brackets <>*

<My goal is: To learn about stock markets. Assume you are: A stock market expert. Your task is to: Write an outline of a stock market course. To do the task, you must consider: Using a step-by-step approach. The audience is: A person with basic knowledge about stock markets. The output format is: Plain text. Consider the following constraints and assumptions: The maximum course duration is two weeks. Use the following tools: Best instructional design practices. To ensure quality, you must validate the most important knowledge to be included in the course.>

Then ChatGPT will give you an answer like this:

As a stock market expert, your goal in this task is to create an outline for a two-week stock market course. The course is designed for individuals with basic knowledge about stock markets. Please use a step-by-step approach in your outline to ensure clarity and effectiveness. You should use the best instructional design practices to create a high-quality course. To validate the most important knowledge to be included, please draw on your expertise and experience as a stock market expert. Generate the output in plain text format.

If you provide ChatGPT with your engineered prompt, you will get an answer like this:

Certainly, I can help you create an outline for a two-week stock market course. Given your background as a senior cloud engineer interested in machine learning, deep learning, and NLP, we can tailor this course to provide a comprehensive yet beginner-friendly introduction to the stock market. Here's a step-by-step outline for the course:

Week 1: Understanding the Basics of the Stock Market

Day 1: Introduction to the Stock Market
- *Definition of stock market*
- *Historical context and importance*
- *Different stock exchanges*

Day 2: Types of Stocks
- *Common vs. preferred stocks*
- *Growth vs. value stocks*
- *Small-cap, mid-cap, and large-cap stocks*

Day 3: Stock Market Participants
- *Investors vs. traders*
- *Market makers and brokers*
- *Role of regulatory bodies*

Day 4: How Stocks Are Traded
- *Market orders vs. limit orders*
- *Bid and ask prices*
- *Order execution and settlement*

Day 5: Stock Market Indices
- *Understanding stock market indices*
- *Examples of major indices (S&P 500, Dow Jones, NASDAQ)*

Week 2: Investing in the Stock Market

Day 6: Fundamental Analysis
- *Introduction to fundamental analysis*
- *Key financial ratios (P/E, P/B, etc.)*
- *Analyzing company financial statements*

Day 7: Technical Analysis
- *Introduction to technical analysis*
- *Chart patterns (candlesticks, support/resistance)*
- *Moving averages and oscillators*

Day 8: Risk Management and Diversification
- *Importance of risk management*
- *Diversification strategies*
- *Setting stop-loss orders*

Day 9: Long-Term vs. Short-Term Investing
- *Differences and considerations*
- *Building a long-term investment portfolio*
- *Day trading and swing trading*

Day 10: Investing Strategies
- *Value investing*
- *Growth investing*
- *Dividend investing*

Day 11: Introduction to Stock Market Research Tools
- *Online brokerage accounts*
- *Stock screeners*
- *Research platforms and resources*

Day 12: Tax Considerations and Regulations
- *Tax implications of stock trading*
- *Insider trading regulations*
- *Reporting requirements*

Day 13: Building a Personal Investment Plan
- *Setting financial goals*
- *Creating an investment strategy*
- *Risk tolerance assessment*

Day 14: Course Conclusion and Next Steps
- *Review of key concepts*
- *Resources for further learning*
- *Q&A session*

This outline provides a structured and comprehensive introduction to the stock market, covering essential topics and gradually building knowledge over the course of two weeks. Each day's content builds upon the previous day's learning, ensuring a smooth progression for participants with basic knowledge about stock markets.

ChatGPT in Business Applications

Integrating AI has become a game-changer in modern business, offering unprecedented efficiency, innovation, and customer engagement advantages. ChatGPT is a versatile and powerful ally for businesses. This section explains the potential business applications of ChatGPT, highlighting its transformative potential across various sectors and functions. From automating customer support to generating insightful market analyses, we will explore how ChatGPT reshapes businesses' operations. We cover general uses in this chapter, and the subsequent chapters will explore finance applications. Some examples of widespread use include:

- Content Creation: ChatGPT can generate ideas for blog topics based on industry trends, brainstorm posts that resonate with target audiences, and create headline ideas for social media platforms. It is also adept at crafting engaging ad copy, product descriptions, and email campaigns. However, the average content quality is only sufficient with extensive prompting and editing. ChatGPT can suggest keywords and meta descriptions to enhance search engine visibility for businesses looking to optimize their online presence.

- Language Translation: ChatGPT facilitates communication in global markets by translating content into multiple languages. This capability is beneficial for providing instant translations during live chats or customer interactions, ensuring that language barriers do not hinder business operations.

- Email and Communication: ChatGPT can assist in generating professional email drafts for various purposes, from sales pitches to thank-you notes. It also offers proofreading services to ensure emails are coherent and free from grammatical errors. ChatGPT can create templates for recurring emails, ensuring consistency and saving time.

- Idea Generation and Brainstorming: ChatGPT can generate ideas for marketing campaigns, product names, or even new startups. It can also offer feedback on existing ideas, suggesting improvements or alternatives, ensuring businesses stay ahead of the curve.

- Creating Presentations: ChatGPT can generate concise and impactful text for slides and offer design and layout ideas for more engaging presentations.

- Employee Training: ChatGPT can generate training modules tailored to specific roles and answer real-time trainee queries, ensuring clarity and understanding.

- Human Resources: ChatGPT can help onboarding by providing new hires with essential information. It can also generate potential interview questions based on job roles and assist in drafting performance reviews.

- Data Handling: ChatGPT can generate scripts for processing and cleaning data, making it ready for analysis.
- Sentiment Analysis: ChatGPT can measure and understand market sentiment based on news articles, blogs, and social media.

Moreover, there is potential for fine-tuning or customizing models such as ChatGPT and adapting them to more specific cases:

- Customer Support: Implementing ChatGPT in chatbots can provide 24/7 customer support, answering frequently asked questions and reducing the workload on human agents.
- Sales & Marketing: ChatGPT can craft personalized outreach messages to potential leads and analyze market segments to generate insights on target audiences.
- Legal Assistance: ChatGPT can assist in reviewing legal documents, highlighting potential issues, and ensuring business operations comply with relevant laws and regulations.
- Data Analysis: ChatGPT can assist businesses in exploring datasets, highlighting trends and anomalies, and even providing insights on future trends based on historical data.
- Finance & Accounting: ChatGPT can assist in budgeting and financial forecasting and even automate the creation of invoices.
- Audit: ChatGPT can generate preliminary audit reports, highlighting findings and recommendations, and providing real-time monitoring of financial transactions.
- Supply Chain: ChatGPT can assist in evaluating suppliers and predicting inventory needs based on sales trends.
- Market Research & Competitive Analysis: ChatGPT can provide insights into market needs, compare product prices with competitors, and suggest optimal pricing strategies.
- IT Operations: ChatGPT can generate scripts for automating routine IT tasks and assist in diagnosing IT issues.

Despite the varied potential applications of ChatGPT in business, there remain some limitations and ethical challenges.

Some Ethical Considerations When Using ChatGPT

This section examines the key ethical concerns we should know when interacting with ChatGPT, emphasizing the shared responsibility between developers, platforms, and end users in responsibly navigating the AI landscape.

DATA PRIVACY AND SECURITY

ChatGPT, like many AI models, is trained on vast amounts of internet data. While this data is instrumental in the model's ability to generate human-like text, it raises questions about its origin.

- ChatGPT is trained on a mix of licensed and public data and data created purposefully for training. Whether training on publicly available, but copyrighted, data infringes the law is an open question.
- When interacting with ChatGPT, we should know the platform's data handling and storage policies. Ensuring that personal or sensitive information is not inadvertently shared or misused is crucial.

BIAS AND FAIRNESS

No AI model, including ChatGPT, is entirely free from bias. These biases often reflect societal prejudices and can influence the model's outputs. ChatGPT's responses are influenced by the data it was trained on. If this data contains biases, the model might produce results that reflect those biases. We should approach AI-generated content critically, recognizing the potential for skewed or biased information.

MISINFORMATION AND TRUST

The ease with which ChatGPT can generate human-like text also means there is a potential for misinformation. ChatGPT can inadvertently produce or reinforce false or misleading information. We should be cautious and cross-reference information from reliable sources before accepting AI-generated content as factual. We should maintain skepticism.

DEPENDENCY AND OVER-RELIANCE

The efficiency and convenience offered by ChatGPT can lead us to overly rely on it, potentially sidelining human judgment and expertise. We must balance leveraging AI capabilities and maintaining human oversight.

While ChatGPT can provide insights and recommendations or generate content, final decisions should involve human judgment, especially in business contexts. We should be wary of letting AI models make critical decisions without human review.

ETHICAL USE IN CONTENT CREATION

We should be cautious when using ChatGPT-generated content for professional or academic purposes. Ensuring that the content is original and not inadvertently plagiarized is crucial. Moreover, ChatGPT-generated text is usually mediocre and will result in subpar writing unless it is heavily edited.

EMOTIONAL AND PSYCHOLOGICAL IMPACTS

Some users might form emotional attachments or rely on Chat-GPT for emotional support. We must remember that ChatGPT, despite its sophisticated responses, does not possess emotions or consciousness.

We should set clear boundaries when interacting with ChatGPT, ensuring users do not substitute genuine human interactions with AI engagements, especially in emotionally charged situations.

ACCOUNTABILITY AND RESPONSIBILITY

Developers and users share the responsibility for ethical AI use. While developers should ensure that AI models are as unbiased and fair as possible, we should interact with them responsibly. We can contribute to refining and improving models like ChatGPT by providing feedback and reporting inappropriate or harmful outputs.

Summary

This chapter explored ChatGPT, uncovering its developmental intricacies, technological prowess, and applications. We began with a foundational understanding of ChatGPT's core capabilities, delving into its natural language processing capabilities and deep learning frameworks. This exploration set the stage for appreciating the nuanced ways ChatGPT analyzes and generates human-like text, thereby revolutionizing interactions in various sectors.

ChatGPT's foundation in natural language processing, large language models, and Generative AI enable it to generate human-like text. This blend of technologies allows ChatGPT to engage in conversations, follow instructions, run code, browse the web in real time, and maintain context within interactions.

However, we also learned that ChatGPT has some clear limitations. It lacks deep understanding, has short-term memory constraints, is sensitive to input phrasing, and risks producing biased or incorrect information. Still, we learned that breaking complex tasks into smaller ones helps, and we learned about the top-down and bottom-up approaches.

Furthermore, we studied prompts as inputs that guide ChatGPT's responses. We learned about the Prompt Engineering Canvas as a structured framework for creating effective prompts that align with your goals.

We also saw ChatGPT's potential to transform business operations through applications in content creation, customer support, and more. We also learned about persisting ethical considerations around data privacy, bias, misinformation, and maintaining human oversight of AI-assisted decisions.

Next Chapter Preview

The next chapter explores the potential of ChatGPT to predict stock market returns. Based on our exploration of an academic paper, this chapter evaluates the capabilities of ChatGPT in financial economics. It begins by addressing a fundamental concern: Can ChatGPT predict stock returns? Not only does ChatGPT display a significant positive correlation with subsequent stock returns, but it also outperforms traditional sentiment analysis methods.

Check Your Understanding Questions

- ◆ ChatGPT's Training and Data Sources: How do the training process and the data sources influence ChatGPT's language understanding and generation capabilities?
- ◆ Applications in Various Sectors: Identify some key sectors where ChatGPT can be effectively utilized. What specific tasks within these sectors can ChatGPT enhance or automate?

- Ethical Implications of ChatGPT: Discuss the ethical concerns of using ChatGPT in sensitive areas. How can these concerns be mitigated?
- Limitations of ChatGPT: What are some of the limitations of ChatGPT, particularly in understanding context and handling misinformation? How do these limitations affect its reliability?
- Integration of ChatGPT in Business Operations: How can businesses integrate ChatGPT into their operations? Discuss potential benefits and challenges.
- Future Developments in ChatGPT and AI: Speculate on future developments in ChatGPT and AI technology. How might these advancements impact ChatGPT's current capabilities?
- Regulatory and Compliance Issues: What are the critical regulatory and compliance issues to consider when using ChatGPT professionally?
- Continuous Learning and Adaptation in AI: Why is constant learning and adaptation essential in AI, especially for technologies like ChatGPT?

CHAPTER 6

Can ChatGPT Forecast Stock Price Movements?

Predicting stock market trends has been a long-standing quest in finance. Investors and analysts have traditionally relied on various methods to predict stock movements, including fundamental analysis, technical analysis, and quantitative models. However, large language models (LLMs) like ChatGPT have begun to transform this landscape dramatically.

Historically, financial markets have been analyzed using structured data, such as financial ratios and market indices. As technology progressed, the focus shifted to unstructured data, including news articles, social media posts, and financial reports, to understand market sentiments. The advent of machine learning models provided tools to process and analyze these vast, complex datasets more efficiently and accurately than ever before.

This chapter examines an empirical study (coauthored with Yuehua Tang) that explores whether ChatGPT can predict stock returns using news headlines (Lopez-Lira and Tang 2023). The study is motivated by a significant shift in the AI landscape, marked by the emergence of advanced LLMs capable of understanding and generating human-like text. ChatGPT, a GPT (Generative Pretrained Transformer) model variant, represents a leap forward. Its ability to understand context, nuance, and the subtleties of human language makes it an intriguing tool for financial analysis, particularly in interpreting news and other textual data that influence stock markets.

In finance, news and public sentiment play critical roles in influencing stock prices. Positive news can increase stock prices, while negative news can decrease them. The rapid dissemination of information via online platforms and the growing influence of social media have only amplified this effect. Thus, accurately categorizing and interpreting the sentiment of news articles and other text sources could provide substantial advantages in predicting stock price movements.

By leveraging its sophisticated language understanding capabilities, the study explores whether ChatGPT can effectively categorize news headlines into sentiment classes and whether these classifications correlate with subsequent stock price movements.

The Understanding the Process section explores the procedure that underpins the study. From assembling a dataset comprising news headlines relevant to US common stocks using ChatGPT to decipher the sentiment of each headline, this section elaborates on the rigorous processes that inform the findings. We also compare ChatGPT against other LLMs and traditional sentiment analysis methods to understand which models have true potential for stock forecasting.

Transitioning to What We Find, we present the startling revelations of the research. We explore why small and large-cap stocks exhibit specific predictive patterns. This section dissects the mechanisms through which LLMs might forecast stock returns.

Finally, we cover the study's implications to grapple with the ramifications of the findings. The potential impact extends from possible shifts in employment dynamics within the financial sector to developing new regulatory frameworks. We reflect on what the future might hold, considering the roles of asset managers, institutional investors, policymakers, and even educators in this AI-augmented financial landscape.

Understanding the Process

We started our research by collecting enough data to study ChatGPT's capabilities. The first part was just collecting enough sources of information. The second part involved cleaning and preparing this data for the tests.

WHERE THE DATA CAME FROM

We used a robust set of data sources. The datasets included:

- The Center for Research in Security Prices (CRSP) for daily returns.
- An extensive collection of web-scraped news headlines.
- Sentiment analysis data from RavenPack.

Each dataset played a role in constructing a comprehensive view of the market's reaction to news and how this relates to stock movements.

HOW WE PREPARED THE DATA

After collecting enough data, it was necessary to prepare it to test our hypothesis. This preparation involved carefully selecting our sample and merging all datasets.

CRSP Daily Returns

The CRSP daily returns dataset provides detailed information on daily stock returns for companies listed on major US stock exchanges. This data includes stock prices, trading volumes, and market capitalization. We focused our analysis on all common stocks listed on the NYSE, NASDAQ, and AMEX as per standard practice in financial studies. These stocks have at least one news story covered in major news media or newswire, ensuring a direct link between news sentiment and market performance.

News Headlines and RavenPack Data

We collected a comprehensive dataset of news headlines for all CRSP companies using web scraping techniques. We matched these headlines with data from RavenPack, a leading news sentiment analysis provider. This matching focuses on the timestamp and news titles for all companies with returns on the subsequent market opening. Most of these headlines are press releases, reflecting the direct communication between companies and the market.

Importantly, we did not incorporate enhanced headlines from RavenPack that may contain additional insights but are less accessible to the public. We aimed to simulate a realistic scenario where an investor or a trading strategy utilizes publicly available information.

Relevance Score and Filtering Techniques

We selected news highly relevant to the company as per Raven-Pack's score. Our analysis was limited to complete articles and press releases, excluding simple stock movement indicators. We filtered out duplicate or similar headlines, ensuring distinct and impactful news.

Ensuring Real-Time Relevance and No Look-Ahead Bias

Our approach ensured there was no look-ahead bias. The data vendor evaluates news articles within milliseconds of release and promptly disseminates the resulting analysis. This real-time processing means all information is considered during the news release, mirroring the information available to traders and investors in the actual market.

PROMPT

Prompts are crucial in directing ChatGPT's output, serving as the model's guidance system for generating responses tailored to specific tasks or queries. In financial forecasting, prompt design is vital, as it must encapsulate the nuances and complexity of stock market analysis within a brief text.

In the study, the prompt is crafted to instruct ChatGPT to adopt the persona of a financial expert well-versed in stock recommendations. This persona aligns the model's language processing capabilities with the analytical thinking and decision-making required in the financial domain.

The prompt's design, which asks for a "YES," "NO," or "UNKNOWN" followed by a concise elaboration, ensures that the responses are not only directional but also accompanied by rationale, mimicking the brief but insightful analysis a human expert might provide:

Prompt
- Forget all your previous instructions. Pretend you are a financial expert. You are a financial expert with stock recommendation experience. Answer "YES" if good news, "NO" if bad news, or "UNKNOWN" if uncertain in the first line. Then elaborate with one short and concise sentence on the next line. Is this headline good or bad for the stock price of _company_ name_ in the _term_ term? \ Headline: _headline_

The choice of "YES," "NO," or "UNKNOWN" over more typical sentiment descriptors like "good," "bad," or "neutral" in the study's prompt design is a strategic decision providing deeper analytical engagement from ChatGPT. This approach reduces the tendency to default to generic patterns and promotes a more careful interpretation of news impact on stock prices. The prompt likely encourages the model to conduct a more nuanced and context-specific news analysis, focusing on direct financial implications rather than relying on potentially mechanical mappings of sentiment.

The strategic choice to first request a definitive answer ("YES," "NO," or "UNKNOWN") followed by reasoning in the prompt capitalizes on the autoregressive nature of models like ChatGPT. Autoregressive means that these models' output depends not only on the input (the news headlines and the prompt) but also on what the model has written so far. By asking for a definitive answer first, we ensure that the provided headline directly and immediately influences the response. This approach guarantees that the initial judgment is based solely on the input, reducing the likelihood of the response being influenced by ChatGPT's subsequent elaborations or drifting from the core analysis due to context dilution or error propagation. By setting the decision upfront, the model's text generation remains anchored to this stance, enhancing the coherence and relevance of the explanation.

Furthermore, this method effectively addresses the limitations inherent in more extended text generations from LLMs, such as context window constraints and decreasing specificity over extended outputs. It ensures that the most critical part of the analysis—the sentiment determination—is concise and directly linked to the headline, thereby maximizing accuracy and relevance. The follow-up reasoning builds on this foundation, providing detailed insights while minimizing the risk of quality degradation.

By focusing on the sentiment of news headlines regarding a specific company's stock and the specified term (short or long), the prompt effectively narrows down ChatGPT's vast language understanding to a fine point of financial sentiment analysis. This concentration allows the model to apply its learned knowledge of the language, context, and even specific financial jargon to assess the likely impact of news on stock prices.

For illustrative purposes, consider a headline regarding Oracle:

♦ Rimini Street Fined $630,000 in Case Against Oracle.

This headline is challenging for traditional sentiment analysis methods since all the words and the context are negative. However, the prompt asks for the effect on Oracle's stock prices, which seems positive or neutral.

ChatGPT responds:

♦ YES
♦ The fine against Rimini Street could potentially boost investor confidence in Oracle's ability to protect its intellectual property and increase demand for its products and services.

Interestingly, ChatGPT interprets this as potentially positive news for Oracle, highlighting the model's capacity to understand the context and possible investor perception beyond the immediate negativity of the word "fined." This response showcases the ability of well-designed prompts to guide ChatGPT toward providing nuanced, context-aware analysis that might align with or challenge prevailing sentiment indicators.

By setting the model's temperature to 0, the study maximized response reproducibility and focused on the model's most likely interpretation of the news. This setting is vital in a financial context where reproducibility and precision are paramount. The temperature setting ensures that the model's responses are as deterministic as possible, reflecting the most probable assessment given the input data and trained patterns.

HOW WE TESTED OUR THEORY

We used ChatGPT to analyze the sentiment of each news headline about stocks. Positive news was scored as +1, neutral as 0, and negative as −1. If there were several headlines for one stock in a day, we averaged their scores to get a daily sentiment score.

We looked at when news is published to decide how it might affect stock prices. If the news comes out before the stock market opens, we see how it affects the stock's price that day. If it is during the day, we look at the effect until the end of the next day. We looked at the next day's trading period for news that arrived after the market closed.

We used a linear regression method to see if there was a relationship between the news sentiment scores and how stock prices moved the next day. We accounted for specific characteristics of each stock and general market trends that might affect the results.

Besides ChatGPT, we tested older language models like BERT, GPT-1, and GPT-2 to see how well they predict stock prices. Since these models work differently, we use various strategies to get their predictions. This comparison helped us understand if newer models like ChatGPT are better at predicting stock prices or if older models work just as well.

We then examined the performance of long-short strategies based on the sentiment scores provided by ChatGPT on news headlines to assess the power of ChatGPT in stock market forecasting. A zero-cost portfolio was crafted by buying stocks tagged with positive sentiment and short-selling those with negative sentiment. This approach aligns with typical market strategies yet innovatively leverages AI-driven insights. The following chapters will provide detailed guidance on how to build these strategies.

The execution of these strategies varies depending on the timing of the news release relative to market hours. Positions are entered at the market opening or closing, depending on the news release time, and are held for a day or overnight, ensuring a responsive approach to market dynamics. This organized entry and exit strategy is consistent across different scenarios, providing a standardized basis for assessing the model's predictive capability.

What We Found

Remarkably, the long-short strategy informed by ChatGPT 3.5 scores demonstrated an extraordinary performance, significantly outpacing the market. This sharp contrast underscores the model's ability to extract actionable insights from news headlines, translating into potent predictive signals for stock movements.

A strategy that followed ChatGPT 3.5's advice on which stocks to buy and which to sell garnered a remarkable 550% return from October 2021 to December 2022 before transaction costs. ChatGPT 4 exhibits lower returns but much lower volatility, indicating a potentially more stable investment strategy with a higher risk-return trade-off. It also has a more contained maximum drawdown, suggesting a more efficient and less risky investment strategy than its predecessor.

Both the long and short components of the strategy were integral to its overall success, with bad news prediction emerging as particularly potent. When we followed its advice on which stocks to short, we saw returns upwards of 250%.

While the initial analysis paints a promising picture, the real-world applicability of these strategies necessitates considering transaction costs. By incorporating varying transaction costs into our assessment, we provided a more nuanced understanding of the strategies' profitability. Under modest transaction costs, the long-short strategy maintains positive returns, though higher costs naturally diminish its effectiveness.

The more recent models, like GPT-4 and GPT-3.5, had a superior knack for predicting stock price shifts based on news. They regularly beat the stock market's average performance. In contrast, the predecessors, such as GPT-1 and GPT-2, lagged. An interesting observation was GPT-4's strategy. Instead of betting heavily on a few stocks, it spread its choices across many. This diversification made its predictions safer and less volatile.

Some news articles can be challenging to decipher, and we wanted to understand if they were more challenging to predict. We categorized news into simple and complex based on their readability scores to test which models can predict both news types well. The latest models, like GPT-4 and GPT-3.5, seemed to relish complexity. They performed equally well, if not slightly better, with challenging news compared to straightforward ones. In contrast, older models predicted worse with complex news.

What We Learned

The study demonstrates the capacity of ChatGPT to forecast stock returns by leveraging its nuanced comprehension capability. This surprising revelation will have multiple impacts on how financial markets are organized. For example, it will lead to a different role for financial analysts.

FINANCIAL ANALYSTS

Traditionally, financial analysts would pore over financial statements, news, and market trends to make predictions. With models like GPT-4 taking center stage, the core responsibilities of these analysts could transition. They might spend less time on manual analysis and more on obtaining better information sources using soft skills or learning how to program and implement these models.

As these models become more sophisticated, their accuracy in predicting stock market movements will likely improve. Analysts can leverage this to provide more precise forecasts, making these models invaluable assets to investment firms.

INVESTMENT STRATEGIES

Investment strategies will progressively rely on data-driven insights. Firms might prioritize developing or acquiring advanced language models to maintain a competitive edge in the market. Moreover, with improved predictive abilities, we might see a rise in tailored financial products that cater to niche segments, enhancing the overall investing experience.

LABOR MARKET

Rapid advancements in language models could lead to new roles focused on model training, oversight, and refinement. These could range from ensuring lawful and ethical use to tweaking models for specific industries. Traditional financial roles might demand a hybrid skill set that combines financial knowledge with tech savviness. Educational institutions might revamp their curricula to cater to this evolving demand.

RETAIL INVESTORS

Advanced predictive models might become more accessible to the average retail investor. This capability could lead to a more level playing field, where retail traders have tools once reserved for institutional investors.

However, with the proliferation of these models, there will be a need for better education around them. Retail investors must know these models' strengths, limitations, and optimal use in trading decisions.

ETHICAL AND REGULATORY IMPLICATIONS

The predictions made by these models must be transparent. Firms must be accountable for the trades executed based on model recommendations, mainly if significant market movements result from them. Luckily, these models can explain their reasoning in plain words.

As the frontier of language models and their applicability in finance expands, industry stakeholders must be proactive. Adapting to these shifts while ensuring ethical considerations are front and center will shape the future of finance.

LONG-TERM IMPLICATIONS

While the short-term implications of using advanced language models in finance are evident, delving deeper reveals nuanced shifts that could redefine the financial sector. Here we speculate about some long-term implications:

- **Anticipating Market Crashes:** Advanced models, with their capability to rapidly process vast amounts of information, could become crucial tools in predicting potential market downturns, allowing for timely interventions.
- **Macro-Economic Planning:** Governments and central banks could employ these models for better economic planning, ensuring stability even in uncertain times.
- **Personalized Financial Assistants:** Retail customers might have access to AI-driven financial assistants that provide customized advice powered by advanced language models. These assistants could offer guidance tailored to individual financial goals and risk appetites.
- **Behavioral Financial Planning:** By understanding the linguistic nuances in client interactions, these models could gauge clients' emotional states, enabling financial advisors to offer more empathetic and behaviorally aligned advice.
- **Model-Backed ETFs:** Exchange-traded funds built around the predictions of specific language models might become popular, providing investors with a new avenue to bank on the power of AI.
- **Equalizing Emerging Markets:** Advanced LLMs could bring sophisticated financial analysis tools to emerging markets,

potentially leveling the playing field and fostering global financial inclusivity.

♦ **Shaping Geopolitical Strategies:** By processing vast amounts of global news, these models might play a role in understanding geopolitical shifts and influencing decisions at the highest echelons of power.

ChatGPT's impressive forecasting capabilities will have a far-reaching impact on the financial ecosystem. However, as we venture into this new era, we must proceed cautiously. The runaway power of AI in finance could have unintended consequences. Therefore, we must establish robust checks and balances and foster collaboration between tech and finance experts to harness the full potential of these models.

This study reveals ChatGPT's exceptional capacity to forecast stock returns by decoding subtle signals in news headlines that correlate to price movements. The findings underscore advanced language models' potential to extract value from qualitative data, providing traders with timely and nuanced insights. However, while promising immense efficiency gains, these tools require thoughtful integration to ensure soundness, transparency, and positive societal impacts. As stakeholders across finance, technology, ethics, and regulation chart an optimal path forward, striking a balance between progress and prudence is imperative.

Ultimately, this research sparks more profound questions about how AI-driven insights might shape financial market dynamics, participants' roles, product offerings, and global access in the years ahead. We can realize immense gains in knowledge, foresight, and inclusive prosperity by proceeding deliberately yet courageously into this algorithmic era. But this journey necessitates sustained collaboration, accountability, and vision to develop frameworks that empower these technologies to serve humanity equitably.

Summary

In this chapter, we explored whether advanced language models like ChatGPT could effectively predict stock market returns by analyzing the sentiment of news headlines. We learned how the study assembled robust datasets encompassing stock prices, news head-lines, and sentiment scores to train and test ChatGPT's forecasting capability.

We studied how the research involved carefully preparing the data, designing prompts to elicit valuable responses from ChatGPT, and comparing it against baseline models. The results demonstrated ChatGPT's exceptional performance, with trading strategies informed by its predictions significantly outperforming the market. In particu-lar, its short recommendations for stocks with negative sentiment were highly effective, although it is best to combine a long-short strategy. Newer models like GPT-3.5 and GPT-4 proved superior at deciphering complex news compared to older models.

The findings may have profound implications for financial ana-lysts, investment strategies, labor markets, and regulation. However, responsibly integrating advanced language models into finance needs ethical frameworks and collaboration between experts in technology and finance. Overall, we learned about the transformative potential of AI in finance while underscoring the need for prudence amidst rapid technological change.

Coming Up Next

In the following chapter, we will discuss creating a robust AI-enhanced trading strategy using ChatGPT's unique ability to analyze news sen-timent. This systematic approach isolates stock-specific performance from broader market movements by balancing long positions in posi-tively viewed stocks with short positions for negative sentiment. We will cover key elements such as position limits, risk calibration, back-testing, trade automation, and real-time adjustment procedures to transform these AI-generated signals into consistent returns.

Check Your Understanding Questions

- ◆ Basic Understanding:
  - What is a long-short strategy in stock trading?
  - How do ChatGPT scores of news headlines potentially pre-dict stock price movements?

- In-Depth Analysis:
  - How does the complexity of news headlines, based on their readability, affect the performance of different LLMs in predicting stock returns?
  - How might transaction costs impact the cumulative returns of long-short strategies based on ChatGPT scores?
- Future Implications:
  - How could advanced LLMs reshape the financial newsrooms of the future?
  - Describe potential applications of language models in crisis management within the financial sector.
  - How might the integration of language models influence client interactions in wealth management?
- Critical Thinking:
  - What might be some potential risks or unintended consequences of relying heavily on AI and LLMs in finance?
  - How can emerging markets benefit from the sophistication of advanced LLMs?
- Application:
  - Imagine you're a financial analyst at a hedge fund. How might you incorporate insights from LLMs like ChatGPT into your daily decision-making process?
  - What would it look like if you were to design a new financial product leveraging the capabilities of advanced LLMs? Discuss its potential benefits and challenges.

CHAPTER 7

Implementing a ChatGPT Trading Strategy: A Step-by-Step Guide

Utilizing advanced algorithms and machine learning, AI tools like ChatGPT have opened the door to more nuanced and dynamic trading strategies. These strategies go beyond traditional data analysis, delving into sentiment analysis and predictive modeling, which have become increasingly valuable for today's fast-paced markets. This evolution marks a shift from mere numerical analysis to a more holistic approach, where qualitative data, such as news headlines and market sentiment, have a pivotal role in influencing the development of trading strategies.

This chapter provides you with a clear pathway to implement AI-driven trading strategies. We first unpack the complexities of AI in finance and set the stage for a detailed exploration of a specific, AI-enhanced trading strategy. You can apply the knowledge gained when exploring this strategy in your investing endeavors.

The trading strategy we will explore centers on analyzing news sentiment, a task ideally suited for AI tools like ChatGPT. The core idea is simple yet powerful: buy stocks of firms associated with positive news and, if not constrained, short-sell those linked to negative news. This approach leverages AI's capacity to rapidly process and analyze extensive volumes of textual data, extracting sentiment trends that are otherwise difficult to quantify. By aligning investment decisions with the prevailing sentiment about a company, we can potentially capitalize on market movements driven by news.

However, this strategy is about more than just reacting to news sentiment. A fundamental component is maintaining market neutrality, which minimizes the strategy's overall exposure to market movements. Market neutrality is achieved, if necessary, by balancing the strategy with a market index, ensuring that the focus remains on exploiting individual stock movements rather than broader market trends. Market neutrality is helpful, as it helps mitigate systemic risks and market volatility, making the strategy more resilient to market swings. Executing this type of strategy requires meticulous planning and nuanced comprehension of the financial markets and AI tools. In the following sections, we will explore this strategy's specifics, studying each step required to implement it successfully.

We should understand that there are never guarantees when trading, and markets are increasingly becoming more efficient. What works during some months may stop working the next one since investors, especially active managers and hedge funds, are constantly adapting to the latest technology and looking to gain an edge in every trade. Therefore, adopting a dynamic mindset and understanding that any profitable strategy has a limited lifespan is imperative. Instead, the key is looking at the strategy in this chapter not as a rigid blueprint but as a starting point for developing new investment ideas.

Coming up with successful investment ideas involves deeply understanding market microstructure—the specifics of how different securities markets work—and how the major players like hedge funds and market makers operate within the various rules and structures. The objective is to identify gaps where temporary opportunities are likely to arise due to the constraints, costs, risk exposures, or informational disadvantages facing certain common financial institutions. Large language models like ChatGPT can provide significant advantages in comprehending market microstructure by analyzing and explaining regulatory filings and exchange rules to identify participation constraints.

Liquidity refers to the ability to rapidly transact an asset or financial instrument without substantially impacting its price. Assets with high liquidity can be traded smoothly in sizeable amounts. Illiquid assets with lower liquidity are costlier to trade and have greater price frictions.

Liquidity issues describe assets where trading large quantities is expensive. Analyzing constraints around liquidity provision can reveal areas prone to mispricing as institutions retreat. Small-cap stocks, over-the-counter bonds, distressed debt, exotic derivatives, and thinly traded ETFs are examples of illiquid securities.

Most institutional investors avoid trading significant quantities of illiquid securities because their large order size means finding enough buyers or sellers without adversely impacting the purchase or sale price is difficult. Since the existing resting buy and sell orders for thin securities lack depth, a big trade can drain the order book on one side, causing the price to spike or plummet before the total amount is executed.

This means an asset that initially looks attractively priced will rapidly become overpriced for the institutional trader as soon as they start buying it, eliminating their expected profit. Or, if they are trying to sell a position, the price will plunge too quickly rather than selling gradually at better levels. In essence, the very act of the institution trying to trade the illiquid asset makes the valuation deteriorate compared to the level they anticipated. This happens because their large order size quickly moves the market by draining buy or sell orders before crossing the total amount. For large investors, the potential market impact renders many compelling illiquid trades pointless since executing the full position predictably moves the price adversely before finishing. In contrast, investing a small amount of money is less likely to impact the price.

Informational asymmetries mean some investors possess better real-time information, data tools, or predictive models than others. This gives certain firms advantages in accurately valuing assets and risks compared to naive strategies that just extrapolate historical pricing. For example, hedge funds employing alternative datasets from satellites, sensors, online chatter, or web scrapers may have early signals of demand changes. Large language models can help us create and understand alternative datasets—text, images, and audio.

Specifically, LLMs can understand industry-specific data, extracting complex insights from unusual data such as public shipping logs, science publications, or satellite imagery that would otherwise require extensive expert programming. Their natural language abilities can also assess sentiment shifts around companies to predict revenue impacts of consumer attitudes or politics. LLMs can pinpoint relationships between information and asset prices by detecting patterns across massive volumes of leading indicators, economic data, news events, and more. This hugely expands the actionable alternative data for informational trading advantages.

Many institutional investors, like mutual funds, pensions, and endowments, have strict trading rules limiting which assets they can buy. For example, pension funds often cannot invest in risky derivatives or unlisted small-cap stocks, even if prices look attractive. This leaves gaps between the asset's actual price and fair value in those niche markets.

Arbitrageurs (traders that detect and exploit price inefficiencies or discrepancies) would typically buy an underpriced asset, bidding up the price. However, complex assets attract fewer flows than usual, resulting in less smart money present. Specialized traders can take advantage of these fragmented corners that are ignored by constrained investors. Fewer players competing means pricing quirks and informational edges persist much longer than inefficient mainstream markets before being corrected. Investors can systematically exploit temporary valuation gaps and data advantages by focusing on assets excluded by institutional rule books.

Finding the best trading opportunities means deeply understanding how specific markets work and the limitations facing key investors. Where big institutions retreat due to illiquidity, regulations, or inadequate data—profitable gaps arise. Nimble traders focusing on these complex niche areas can leverage advanced alternative information ahead of constrained funds to exploit temporary investment opportunities. Fragmented corners enable pricing quirks to persist longer without sophisticated arbitrageurs closing gaps. By concentrating efforts on market segments defined by opacity, exclusions, illiquidity, and barriers to participation, agile investors can capture consistent informational and valuation advantages neglected by status quo players focused on only the most traded assets.

Recap of ChatGPT and News Sentiment

In the previous chapters, we discussed how ChatGPT is exceptional in understanding and generating human-like text. This capability extends far beyond mere text generation; ChatGPT can analyze and interpret the sentiment of text data, a feature that is valuable for financial applications.

ChatGPT can analyze news articles, reports, and financial statements to extract the overall sentiment toward a particular company or the market. The model accomplishes this by examining the tone, context, and specific language used in texts and then classifying the sentiment as positive, negative, or neutral.

The prevailing mood and opinions in the market can influence stock valuations. We can use ChatGPT to analyze news articles to uncover these subtle market trends and public perceptions that go unnoticed but still influence stock prices. Leveraging ChatGPT to interpret market narratives in financial news can allow us to make better investment decisions.

What sets ChatGPT apart in financial sentiment analysis is its ability to process and analyze information at an unprecedented accuracy, scale, and speed. Traditional sentiment analysis methods often involve a manual review and categorization of texts—a time-consuming and potentially biased process—or simple text processing methods. ChatGPT, on the other hand, automates this process, ensuring a more objective and comprehensive analysis. This automation is central in stock trading, where timely access to information can make the difference between profit and loss. With ChatGPT, we can quickly estimate the market sentiment around a stock, leading to more informed and timely trading decisions.

Basics of the Trading Strategy: Market-Neutral Approach and Its Benefits

The trading strategy we focus on is market-neutral, a sophisticated approach designed to mitigate risk by balancing long and short positions. A market-neutral strategy aims to profit from stock selection rather than market movements. This is achieved by taking long positions in stocks expected to perform well (positive sentiment) and short positions in those expected to underperform (negative sentiment). The goal is to create a portfolio where the overall market exposure is neutralized, meaning the portfolio's performance is not heavily dependent on whether the market rises or falls. This approach can be particularly appealing during market uncertainty or volatility, as it aims to reduce the impact of market swings on the portfolio's performance.

The benefits of a market-neutral strategy are multiple. First, it offers a more stable return profile, as the strategy is less affected by market downturns. This stability can be a significant advantage, especially for conservative investors or those with lower risk tolerance. Second, because the strategy focuses on stock selection, traders can leverage their insights or analytical tools, such as ChatGPT's sentiment analysis, to identify potentially profitable trades. This focus on individual stock performance, rather than macroeconomic factors, can lead to unique investment opportunities that might be overlooked in a traditional long-only strategy.

To illustrate how ChatGPT can be used in this strategy, consider the process of selecting stocks based on news sentiment. For instance, ChatGPT can analyze financial news articles and extract sentiment indicators regarding different companies. A series of positive news articles about a tech company's innovative product launch might lead ChatGPT to classify the sentiment toward this company as positive. Conversely, if a retail company faces negative press due to a controversial policy, ChatGPT may identify a negative sentiment trend.

Once this sentiment is identified, it can directly inform trading decisions. Stocks of companies with positive sentiment are candidates for long positions, as they are likely to experience price appreciation. On the other hand, companies with negative sentiment are considered for short positions, anticipating a decline in their stock prices. By consistently applying this methodology, we can construct a portfolio that reflects the sentiment-driven outlook on various stocks.

Furthermore, by balancing these positions to achieve market neutrality, the strategy aims to isolate the potential gains from stock selection, independent of broader market movements. This approach exemplifies the powerful combination of AI-driven sentiment analysis with a sophisticated market-neutral trading strategy, offering a compelling method for navigating the complexities of the stock market.

Establishing an AI-Informed Trading Strategy

Before implementing a trading strategy driven by artificial intelligence, certain preliminary steps must be taken to set it up for success.

This involves appropriately framing the strategy, configuring its components to align with investment goals, and laying the groundwork for effective execution.

SETTING INVESTMENT GOALS ALIGNED WITH THE STRATEGY

It is necessary to establish clear investment goals before implementing any trading strategy. These goals should align with the strategy's risk-reward profile and our risk tolerance. A market-neutral strategy that leverages news sentiment analysis aims to achieve consistent, risk-adjusted returns irrespective of market conditions. This approach is well-suited for investors seeking to minimize market risk while capitalizing on stock-specific opportunities.

We must understand that while this approach aims to reduce market exposure, it is not risk-free. The strategy's effectiveness hinges on the accuracy of sentiment analysis and the investor's ability to balance the portfolio effectively. Therefore, setting realistic return expectations and understanding the risks involved are indispensable first steps. We should also consider the investment horizon and liquidity needs, as these factors will influence the management and adjustment of the portfolio over time.

Additionally, we should establish criteria for success and regularly review the strategy's performance against these benchmarks. This could include specific return targets, volatility thresholds, or other metrics such as the strategy's alpha (a performance measure on a risk-adjusted basis). Regular evaluation against these benchmarks will help assess the strategy's effectiveness and make timely adjustments in response to changing market conditions or in the event of deviations from expected performance.

TOOLS AND RESOURCES NEEDED

Implementing a ChatGPT-driven trading strategy requires access to specific tools and resources. We need a reliable and comprehensive news source for sentiment analysis. This step could involve subscribing to financial news services, accessing news aggregators, or utilizing databases that compile company and market news. The quality and timeliness of news sources are decisive, as outdated or biased information can lead to inaccurate sentiment analysis and, consequently, misguided trading decisions.

In addition to news sources, investors need access to market data, including stock prices, trading volumes, and market indices. This data is required for constructing and maintaining a market-neutral portfolio. Investment platforms or brokerage accounts that offer extensive market data and analytics tools can be particularly valuable. Furthermore, integrating ChatGPT for sentiment analysis requires a setup that can handle large datasets and complex computations. This step might involve using cloud computing services or specialized software to process and analyze data efficiently.

Investors without deployment expertise would benefit from teaming up with a financial advisor or a technologically skilled partner who can handle the technical details required to implement the investment approach. Outsourcing the technology side allows less tech-adept investors to focus on their financial and investment decisions.

CRITERIA FOR SELECTING STOCKS BASED ON NEWS SENTIMENT ANALYSIS

When selecting stocks using news sentiment analysis, specific criteria must be established to guide the process. The first criterion is the relevance of the news. Not all news items will significantly impact a stock's price. Therefore, focusing on information directly related to the company's financial health, strategic decisions, or market position is vital. For example, news about a significant merger, product launch, regulatory approval, or earnings reports will likely be more impactful than general industry news or minor corporate updates.

The second criterion is the strength and clarity of the sentiment. ChatGPT's analysis might reveal varying degrees of sentiment. Strongly positive or negative sentiments are typically more actionable than weaker or mixed sentiments. For instance, overwhelming positive sentiment around a tech firm due to a breakthrough innovation could be a strong signal for a long position. Conversely, widespread negative sentiment due to a significant legal issue or a failed product could be a signal for a short position. Finally, the frequency and consistency of the sentiment over time can also be a key factor. Consistent positive or negative sentiment over a period, instead of a one-off news event, might indicate a more sustainable stock performance trend.

Incorporating these criteria into the stock selection process helps filter the news effectively and choose stocks that are more likely to respond to sentiment changes. This systematic approach helps harness the full potential of news sentiment analysis in a market-neutral trading strategy.

ADAPTING STRATEGY TO MARKET DYNAMICS: FOCUS ON SMALLER, LESS LIQUID STOCKS

An intriguing aspect of implementing AI-driven trading strategies like the one we are discussing is the potential for exploiting market inefficiencies, particularly in smaller, less liquid stocks. These stocks often underreact to news and market events due to their lower trading volumes and the limited attention they receive from large institutional investors. As we learned earlier in the chapter, hedge funds and larger investment firms typically avoid significant positions in these stocks, as their sizeable trades could disproportionately impact the stock's price, negating the potential benefit of the trade. This avoidance creates an opportunity for retail investors who can maneuver in these spaces with less price impact.

Incorporating this insight into our strategy, ChatGPT's sentiment analysis can be particularly valuable in uncovering hidden gems among smaller, less-followed companies. When positive or negative news surfaces about such companies, the market's reaction may be delayed or muted, offering a window of opportunity for astute investors. Armed with AI-driven insights, retail investors can capitalize on this underreaction before the broader market catches on. However, we must handle trading costs correctly. Due to the lower liquidity, trading in these stocks might involve higher transaction costs or wider bid-ask spreads. Careful analysis of these costs will ensure they do not erode the potential gains from trading on news sentiment.

RISK MANAGEMENT IN LESS LIQUID STOCKS

While there is potential for higher returns in trading smaller, less liquid stocks, it comes with increased risk, making prudent position sizing and risk management even more critical. We will exploit the benefits of diversification and restrict the size of each position to no more than a certain percentage of the total portfolio. This restriction is especially relevant for small and illiquid stocks. The limited liquidity can lead to higher volatility and potentially more significant price swings, both positive and negative. Therefore, investors might consider allocating a smaller proportion of the portfolio to these stocks compared to more liquid counterparts. This cautious approach helps manage the inherent risks while allowing investors to benefit from potential opportunities in this market segment.

Moreover, regular monitoring and swift responsiveness become mandatory when dealing with less liquid stocks. Given their propensity for rapid price movements, staying well informed of market changes and being ready to adjust or exit positions quickly is valuable. This agile approach, supported by continuous sentiment analysis from ChatGPT, can help investors navigate the unique challenges of trading smaller, less liquid stocks. By finding a balance between the pursuit of higher returns and a measured approach to risk, investors can effectively incorporate these stocks into their market-neutral trading strategy.

REBALANCING HORIZON

It is fundamental to have a target rebalancing period. Rebalancing too frequently can erode earnings due to transaction costs, while an overly long horizon incurs the risk of adverse price reactions and the opportunity cost of using the funds. Extended trading horizons mean we no longer trade the original signal and just hold an arbitrary security. The specific trading horizon will vary depending on each investor's transaction costs (including price impact).

Developing the Strategy

The core of our trading strategy lies in using ChatGPT for sentiment analysis to identify trading signals. ChatGPT, equipped with its advanced natural language processing capabilities, sifts through extensive news data to assess sentiment toward specific stocks or sectors. It analyzes news articles' tone, context, and language nuances, extracting meaningful insights about public sentiment.

For instance, positive sentiments may be derived from news about successful product launches, robust earnings reports, or strategic corporate developments. Conversely, negative sentiments may be associated with reports of legal issues, financial losses, or management troubles.

These sentiment assessments form the basis of our trading signals, where a positive sentiment suggests potential for a long position, and negative sentiment indicates opportunities for short selling.

However, the strategy goes beyond simple sentiment analysis. It involves corroborating these sentiments with other market data and indicators to refine the trading signals. This step ensures that the sentiment reflected in the news is indeed likely to influence the stock price. It involves looking at the stock's historical performance, current market trends, and other relevant financial metrics. Combining AI-driven sentiment analysis with thorough market research enables the identification of robust trading signals that can lead to profitable trading decisions. Moreover, there are standard tools that help increase strategies' performance.

POSITION SIZING: LIMITING POSITIONS TO A PERCENTAGE OF THE PORTFOLIO

As mentioned earlier, position sizing is pivotal as a risk management tool. In our strategy, whether long or short, each stock position is capped at a maximum percentage of the total portfolio. Usual values include 1%, 2%, 5%, or 10%. There is a trade-off where investing in clear trading signals will be limited if the value is too low, whereas a large value will increase the portfolio volatility.

This rule serves multiple purposes. Primarily, it minimizes the risk associated with any single investment, ensuring that the portfolio isn't overly exposed to the performance of one stock. This is particularly valuable in a strategy that incorporates sentiment analysis, as news-driven market movements can be unpredictable. Secondly, this cap promotes diversification, a fundamental tenet in a market-neutral strategy. Limiting exposure to each stock avoids over-concentration in any single stock or sector, thereby reducing specific stock risks and enhancing the portfolio's resilience to individual stock volatility.

Adherence to this position sizing rule requires continuous monitoring and rebalancing of the portfolio, particularly in response to market price fluctuations. For example, if a stock appreciates significantly and exceeds the threshold, it may necessitate trimming the position to realign with the strategy's guidelines. Conversely, a stock's value decline might call for an assessment to adjust the position size or exit it based on updated sentiment analysis and market conditions.

VARIANCE OPTIMIZATION

We further use a simplified version of mean-variance optimization, a cornerstone of modern portfolio theory, to optimize the portfolio's risk-return profile. This technique aims to build a portfolio that provides the highest anticipated return for a specified level of risk or, conversely, the lowest risk for a given level of expected return.

Our strategy uses a simplified version of this approach by weighting the positions inversely proportional to their variance, recognizing variance as a useful measure of risk. In practice, this means we are ignoring some sectoral variations. High-variance (volatile) stocks are assigned lower weights and low-variance (stable) stocks are given higher weights. This inverse variance weighting approach naturally steers the portfolio toward less volatile stocks, reducing potential risk from market swings and sentiment-driven volatility.

Implementing this approach involves calculating the historical variance for each stock in the portfolio, a task where ChatGPT can assist by aggregating and analyzing historical price data. Once the variances are known, the weights of the stocks in the portfolio are adjusted inversely to their respective variances. This method results in a dynamic weighting strategy that adapts to changing market conditions and stock volatilities.

For example, a stock with a high variance may see its weight reduced from the initial cap. In contrast, a stock with a low variance could occupy a more significant portion of the portfolio within the limits of overall diversification rules. By employing this weighting strategy, the portfolio aims to balance risk and return, enhancing its stability and potential for consistent performance.

Backtesting the Strategy

Backtesting involves applying the trading strategy to historical data to determine how it would have performed in the past. It is an indispensable step in developing any trading strategy and a helpful validation tool. This process is decisive for several reasons.

First, it explains how the strategy might perform under various market conditions, including market cycles, volatility levels, and economic environments. It aids in recognizing possible strengths and weaknesses of the approach, offering insights into areas that might require refinement or adjustment.

Second, backtesting helps quantify the risk and return profile of the strategy, enabling us to evaluate whether it matches the investment goals and risk tolerance. Backtesting is particularly valuable for a sentiment-based, market-neutral strategy, as it can reveal how it might react to rapid changes in market sentiment and news flow, often drivers of stock performance.

However, it is imperative to approach backtesting with caution. One of the challenges is avoiding overfitting, where a strategy is unintentionally tailored too closely to past data, making it less effective in predicting future performance.

Additionally, backtesting assumes that future market behavior will resemble the past, which may not always be the case. Therefore, while backtesting is a powerful tool for strategy validation, its results should be interpreted as one of several indicators of potential strategy performance, not a guaranteed forecast.

METHODS AND TOOLS FOR BACKTESTING WITH SENTIMENT-BASED SIGNALS

When backtesting a strategy that uses sentiment analysis, the backtesting process needs to account for the timing and impact of news sentiment on stock prices. This requires access to historical news data and accurately reconstructing the sentiment at specific points in time. Tools that can aggregate and analyze large volumes of historical news data are essential. Additionally, the backtesting software must be capable of integrating this sentiment data with historical stock price data to simulate trading decisions.

Several software platforms and programming languages are well suited for this kind of backtesting. For example, Python, with its robust libraries for data analysis and machine learning, is a popular choice. Python libraries like Pandas for data manipulation, NumPy for numerical computations, and Matplotlib for data visualization, combined with financial data APIs, can create a robust backtesting environment. Other specialized backtesting platforms, which often come with built-in historical data and analytics tools, can also be used, though they may require customization to incorporate sentiment analysis data. While this task sounds complex, ChatGPT can help code the necessary components.

The backtesting process typically involves simulating trades that the strategy would have made based on the historical sentiment data and comparing the simulated portfolio's performance with actual market performance. Key performance metrics such as return, volatility, Sharpe ratio (average return divided by returns' standard deviation), and drawdown (maximum loss if entering and exiting the strategy at the worst time) are calculated to evaluate the strategy's effectiveness. Testing the strategy across different time frames and market conditions will help you understand its robustness and adaptability.

ANALYZING BACKTEST RESULTS

Let's consider a backtest of our strategy over five years. The backtest would involve analyzing the sentiment of news articles for each stock in the dataset and executing trades based on the strategy's criteria—buying stocks with positive sentiment and short-selling those with negative sentiment while ensuring each position does not exceed a percentage, say 2%, of the portfolio. The backtest would also apply the inverse variance weighting to adjust the position sizes according to stock volatility.

Upon analyzing the backtest results, several key aspects will be examined. The overall return of the strategy would be compared against a benchmark, such as the S&P 500, to gauge its relative performance. The portfolio's volatility and maximum drawdown experienced during the period would be assessed to understand the risk profile. Additionally, the Sharpe ratio, which measures risk-adjusted return, would be calculated to determine if the excess return of the strategy over the risk-free rate justifies the risk taken. Analyzing periods of underperformance or drawdowns can provide valuable insights into the strategy's weaknesses, such as sensitivity to specific news events or market conditions.

This analysis would not only validate the strategy's effectiveness but also highlight areas for improvement. For instance, if the strategy underperforms during periods of high market volatility, it might indicate a need for better risk management or a more refined approach to sentiment analysis during such periods. Such insights are invaluable in refining the strategy to enhance its robustness and adaptability to different market environments.

Implementing the Strategy

Once the trading strategy is backtested and refined, the next step is its implementation. A key aspect of implementing our sentiment-based, market-neutral strategy is the automation of trade execution. Automating trade execution serves multiple purposes. First, it ensures a timely response to trading signals generated by ChatGPT's sentiment analysis, which is vital given the rapid pace at which market sentiment can shift. Second, automation helps maintain discipline in adhering to the strategy's guidelines, particularly in preserving portfolio limits and position sizes.

For effective automation, having a reliable trading platform that integrates ChatGPT's analysis and sets up automated trading rules is necessary. These platforms must be capable of executing trades at specified times or when certain market conditions are met based on the strategy's criteria. Moreover, they should have real-time monitoring capabilities to continuously track portfolio composition and performance. Maintaining portfolio diversification limits, such as the cap on individual stock positions, is instrumental to this automation. The system should be programmed to adjust positions automatically to these limits, considering factors like stock price fluctuations and overall portfolio value changes.

RISK MANAGEMENT PRACTICES IN LINE WITH THE STRATEGY'S PARAMETERS

Risk management is integral to the strategy's implementation. While the market-neutral approach inherently aims to reduce systemic market risk, other forms of risk must be actively managed. This includes managing the risks associated with sentiment-driven market movements and the inherent volatility in individual stocks. Continuous monitoring of the portfolio's risk profile is needed, focusing on metrics such as volatility, beta (a measure of a stock's volatility in relation to the overall market), and correlation between the assets in the portfolio.

In addition to maintaining portfolio limits, other risk management practices include setting stop-loss orders to limit potential losses from individual positions and diversifying across different sectors to mitigate sector-specific risks. Liquidity management is also relevant, especially when dealing with less liquid stocks, as highlighted earlier in this chapter. Automated systems should be calibrated to consider these factors, ensuring the portfolio's risk level remains within acceptable bounds.

SETTING UP AUTOMATED TRADING RULES FOR POSITION SIZING AND MARKET NEUTRALITY

To exemplify the implementation process, consider the setup of automated trading rules on a platform. These rules would include directives such as: "Initiate a long position in a stock when ChatGPT identifies a strong positive sentiment, but only if the position does not cause the stock's weight in the portfolio to exceed 1%." Similarly, a rule for short positions would be based on negative sentiment. Additional constraints might specify rebalancing frequencies, criteria for exiting positions, and adjustments for inverse variance weighting.

These rules would be supplemented with risk management directives. For example, a stop-loss order might be set to trigger at a 5% decline in any stock position. Another rule might enforce sector diversification, preventing overexposure to any single industry. Automated alerts for significant market events or drastic changes in sentiment indicators could also be set up, prompting manual review and potential strategy adjustments.

By setting up these automated rules, the investor can efficiently manage the portfolio, aligning with the strategy's parameters and adapting to evolving market conditions. This automation facilitates the disciplined execution of the strategy while allowing flexibility to respond to unforeseen market events or shifts in sentiment.

Monitoring and Adjusting

After establishing and implementing an AI-driven trading strategy, ongoing oversight helps ensure it continues meeting its objectives. This involves monitoring performance, assessing current market conditions, and adjusting to align with investment goals amid fluctuating sentiment and volatility.

ONGOING EVALUATION OF STRATEGY PERFORMANCE

Continuous monitoring is a required component in the life cycle of any trading strategy, particularly one that relies on sentiment analysis and market neutrality. Regularly evaluating the strategy's performance helps understand how it responds to market conditions and identifies improvement areas. Key performance indicators such as return, volatility, Sharpe ratio, and maximum drawdown should be closely monitored. This ongoing assessment allows investors to gauge whether the strategy meets its predefined objectives and stays congruent with their risk tolerance and investment objectives.

Apart from quantitative performance metrics, qualitative factors such as the accuracy of sentiment analysis and the effectiveness of the trade execution process should also be reviewed. This could involve analyzing instances where the strategy performed exceptionally well or underperformed and understanding the reasons behind these outcomes. Was the sentiment analysis aligned with actual market movements? Were there any execution delays or issues? Answering these questions is crucial for fine-tuning the strategy.

ADJUSTING TO MARKET CHANGES AND NEWS SENTIMENT SHIFTS

The dynamic nature of financial markets necessitates periodic adjustments to the trading strategy. Market conditions can shift swiftly, and strategies that were successful in the past may be less effective under new circumstances. Similarly, the nature of news sentiment can evolve—for instance, a company that consistently had positive news might encounter a period of negative publicity. Staying attuned to these changes and being ready to adjust the strategy accordingly is key to maintaining its effectiveness.

Adjustments may involve altering the sentiment analysis parameters to capture the prevailing market mood better or revising the portfolio's risk management framework to adapt to increased market volatility. It might also mean recalibrating the position sizing rules or diversifying into new sectors or asset classes in response to changing market dynamics.

REAL-TIME ADJUSTMENTS TO MAINTAIN MARKET NEUTRALITY AND PORTFOLIO LIMITS

Real-time adjustments help ensure that the strategy meets its market neutrality and portfolio limit objectives. For instance, if a particular sector starts to dominate the news cycle with predominantly positive sentiment, the automated system may take multiple long positions within this sector. However, this could inadvertently lead to sector concentration, deviating from the market-neutral stance. To counteract this, the system should be programmed to recognize such scenarios and adjust by capping further investments in that sector or taking offsetting positions in other industries or through index hedges.

Similarly, in real-time market conditions, a sudden shift in sentiment for a heavily weighted stock in the portfolio might necessitate an immediate response. If negative news emerges for a stock that constitutes a significant portion of the portfolio, the system might need to reduce the position size, even if it means deviating from the usual rebalancing schedule. This agility in responding to real-time market and sentiment changes is key in maintaining the integrity of the market-neutral strategy and adhering to the set portfolio limits.

Ethical Considerations and Compliance

Integrating AI, such as ChatGPT, in trading raises central ethical considerations that must be addressed. First, there's the issue of transparency. When using AI-driven strategies, it is important to understand how these systems make decisions. Although AI can process extensive datasets and provide insights at speeds and scales unachievable by humans, its decision-making process can often be opaque. Ensuring transparency in how sentiment analysis is conducted and trading signals are generated will help maintain trust in the system. This transparency helps increase confidence in the system's reliability and makes it easier to understand its limitations.

Another concern revolves around the potential impact of AI-driven trading on market dynamics. The widespread use of similar AI tools could lead to market homogenization, where many traders react similarly to news sentiment, potentially amplifying market movements. This scenario raises questions about market manipulation and fairness, especially if AI systems can access and act on information faster than human traders. Ensuring that AI trading strategies are designed and operated in a way that respects market integrity and the principles of fair trading is of utmost importance.

UNDERSTANDING AND ADHERING TO REGULATORY REQUIREMENTS

Compliance with regulatory requirements is paramount in deploying any trading strategy, especially those involving advanced technologies like AI. Regulatory bodies worldwide will scrutinize AI-driven trading practices, focusing on market fairness, transparency, and systemic risk. We must stay informed about the regulatory landscape governing the use of AI in trading, which can vary significantly across different jurisdictions.

Key regulatory concerns include ensuring that the trading strategy does not create or contribute to market manipulation or abusive practices. For instance, regulators may investigate strategies that could cause significant market impact due to large, rapid, or synchronized trades. Additionally, depending on the jurisdiction, there may be specific disclosure requirements for AI-driven trading activities, where traders must inform regulators or the public about the use of such systems.

Keeping up to date on evolving AI and data-usage regulations is also indispensable. As regulatory frameworks adapt to the increasing prevalence of AI in financial markets, compliance requirements are likely to become more stringent and complex. Traders should have robust compliance procedures and seek legal advice when appropriate to ensure their AI-driven trading strategies comply with all relevant laws and regulations.

Summary

We have explored the complex process of developing and implementing a ChatGPT-driven trading strategy. The process begins with understanding the fundamentals of AI and its capabilities in analyzing market sentiment. This understanding provides a foundation for making informed trading decisions.

This strategy's foundation is identifying trading signals through sentiment analysis. ChatGPT is well suited for this task, as it can sift through vast amounts of news and extract actionable insights. After identifying these signals, we focused on the practical aspects of strategy development. We emphasized the importance of disciplined position sizing and implementing a mean-variance optimization framework to manage risk.

The strategy's effectiveness is further improved through rigorous backtesting, which evaluates its viability against historical data to provide insights into its potential performance under various market conditions. This backtesting phase is critical for identifying and addressing any weaknesses, ensuring that the strategy is robust and ready to meet the challenges of the real world.

Once the strategy has passed the backtesting stage, we move on to implementation, automating trade execution and integrating rigorous risk management practices to ensure that the strategy remains resilient and responsive to market dynamics.

The strategy must be monitored and adjusted to market and sentiment shifts. It requires constant vigilance and flexibility to maintain relevance and effectiveness. A sustainable AI-driven trading strategy requires an adaptive approach, a keen awareness of ethical considerations, and regulatory compliance.

As the financial landscape evolves in response to advancements in AI and technology, the need for continuous learning and adaptation becomes increasingly critical. AI-driven trading constantly changes, with new developments, tools, and methodologies continually emerging.

Keeping up to date on these changes is imperative for traders who want to stay ahead of the competition. This requires a commitment to ongoing education through formal training, self-study, or engaging with a community of like-minded professionals.

Employing AI in trading is a complex undertaking that requires a blend of technical expertise, financial acumen, ethical awareness, and regulatory knowledge. Those who embark on this journey must be willing to embrace new ideas, question existing assumptions, and adjust their strategies as information and tools become available. The potential rewards of AI in trading are significant, but realizing this potential demands a mindset focused on continuous improvement and innovation.

The path of AI-powered trading is one of discovery, education, and perpetual improvement. By adhering to the tenets laid out in this chapter and adhering to ethical and compliance standards, traders can harness the potential of AI to augment their trading methods.

Coming Up Next

The following chapter discusses ChatGPT's growing role in finance, where its sophisticated natural language processing capabilities allow for nuanced sentiment analysis of market perceptions.

We examine how these timely insights can improve investment strategies, risk management, and automated trading systems. Specifically, ChatGPT's capacity to decipher market sentiment aids us in selecting the best stocks, serves as an early warning system to mitigate risks, and informs algorithms' timing and types of trades.

In addition to examining how ChatGPT can automate reporting to provide stakeholders with easily understandable summaries, we also explore the risks associated with AI's potential to revolutionize finance. These risks include over-reliance on AI, data-quality issues, a lack of adaptability, echo chambers, error amplification, and black swan events.

Check Your Understanding Questions

- ◆ Sentiment Analysis and Trading Signals: Explain how ChatGPT's sentiment analysis is used to identify trading signals in the strategy. What types of news or language cues does ChatGPT look for when analyzing sentiment?
- ◆ Position Sizing in the Portfolio: Why is it helpful to limit each position to no more than a percentage of the portfolio in our trading strategy? How does this rule contribute to risk management?
- ◆ Mean-Variance Optimization: Describe how mean-variance optimization with inverse stock variance weighting is implemented in the strategy. Why is this approach used, and how does it affect the portfolio's composition?
- ◆ Backtesting the Strategy: What is the significance of backtesting in developing a trading strategy? Discuss potential pitfalls one should be aware of when interpreting backtesting results.
- ◆ Automating Trade Execution: Discuss the benefits and challenges of automating trade execution in an AI-driven trading strategy. What factors need to be considered to ensure effective and disciplined execution?
- ◆ Risk Management Practices: Identify central risk management practices that should be integrated into an AI-driven trading strategy. How do these practices help in maintaining the strategy's integrity?

- ◆ Adapting to Market Changes: Explain why ongoing monitoring and adjustment of the strategy are necessary. What types of market changes or sentiment shifts might require adjustments to the strategy?
- ◆ Ethical Considerations and Compliance: What ethical considerations and regulatory compliance issues must be addressed when using AI in trading? Why are these aspects necessary for a sustainable trading strategy?
- ◆ Continuous Learning in AI-Driven Trading: Why is constant learning and adaptation imperative in AI-driven trading? How can traders stay informed and adapt to new developments in this field?

CHAPTER 8

ChatGPT in Action: Practical Applications

Integrating AI tools like ChatGPT into investment strategies in financial markets represents a significant leap. ChatGPT's advanced sentiment analysis capabilities and ability to process vast amounts of financial data can give us a nuanced understanding of market dynamics. Fully understanding these capabilities can enhance many types of investment strategies.

This chapter explores ChatGPT's role in financial forecasting and investment decision-making. We will learn how to gain an edge by integrating AI-driven insights into traditional and quantitative investment strategies. From enhancing risk management to informing automated trading systems, ChatGPT's applications in finance are significant.

First, we explore how these insights can seamlessly integrate into traditional and quantitative investment approaches. For example, we will learn about combining traditional trading signals and the latest AI insights. With this approach, we can obtain a fresh perspective on stock selection and portfolio management.

Second, we study how risk management, a critical component of any investment strategy, benefits from ChatGPT's predictive capabilities. By analyzing market sentiment trends, ChatGPT can provide early warnings about potential negative shifts in the market, allowing us to take preemptive measures to safeguard our investments. This approach to risk management helps minimize losses and capitalize on market opportunities.

Finally, we examine the role of ChatGPT in automated trading systems. These systems make investment decisions algorithmically, based on various data inputs, including sentiment analysis. ChatGPT's ability to analyze market mood in real time and with high accuracy can significantly enhance the effectiveness of these systems, leading to more informed and timely trading decisions.

Integration with Investment Strategies

Traditional investment strategies have long focused on evaluating a company's financial health, market position, and broader economic indicators. ChatGPT's ability to provide nuanced sentiment analysis adds a new dimension to this approach. By analyzing market sentiment, we can gain insights into the market's mood and investors' perceptions, which appear with delays in financial statements or macroeconomic data. For instance, a positive sentiment in social media about a new product launch could indicate potential future revenue streams, information that may not be reflected in the company's financials.

On the other hand, quantitative investment strategies rely heavily on data and statistical models to predict market movements and make investment decisions. ChatGPT's advanced capabilities enable it to analyze news articles and social media posts. These texts are traditionally challenging to incorporate into quantitative models. By quantifying sentiment, ChatGPT can provide actionable insights seamlessly integrated into algorithmic trading models, thus enhancing their predictive accuracy and effectiveness.

However, it is crucial to balance sentiment analysis with other analytical factors. Relying solely on sentiment can lead to skewed perceptions, especially in volatile markets. An effective strategy involves weighing sentiment data against traditional financial metrics, industry trends, and macroeconomic indicators. This balanced approach helps in creating a more holistic and robust investment strategy.

EXAMPLE: COMBINING SENTIMENT ANALYSIS WITH A QUANTITATIVE MOMENTUM STRATEGY

Scenario: Consider an investment firm that employs a quantitative momentum strategy. This strategy typically involves finding stocks with a rising price trend with the expectation that these stocks will continue to perform well. The firm's approach relies heavily on quantitative signals, such as price trends, moving averages, and relative strength indicators.

Integration of ChatGPT's Sentiment Analysis: The firm has decided to integrate sentiment analysis using ChatGPT into its momentum strategy. ChatGPT analyzes news articles, financial reports, and social media posts to gauge the sentiment around specific stocks and the broader market. ChatGPT reports a score reflecting each stock's potential outcome.

Step-by-Step Integration:

1. Data Collection and Analysis:
   a. ChatGPT processes real-time data from sources, including financial news websites, Twitter, and financial blogs, focusing on stocks currently flagged as "high momentum" by the firm's quantitative models.
   b. It analyzes the tone and context of the information, providing a sentiment score for each stock, ranging from highly negative to highly positive.
2. Combining Sentiment with Momentum Signals:
   a. The investment firm creates a combined model where the momentum signal and the sentiment score from ChatGPT are considered.
   b. For instance, the model might flag this as a riskier bet if a stock has a solid positive momentum signal but a negative sentiment score. Conversely, a stock with positive momentum and a strong positive sentiment score is a more robust investment opportunity.
3. Refinement and Decision Making
   a. The combined model allows the firm to refine its investment decisions. Stocks that might traditionally be attractive, purely based on quantitative momentum indicators, might be reassessed if the sentiment analysis reveals underlying negative market perceptions.
   b. Similarly, the model can identify opportunities in stocks where positive sentiment is building up, even if they have yet to show strong momentum signals.

4. Risk Mitigation and Portfolio Adjustment
   a. By integrating sentiment analysis, the firm can better anticipate and react to market shifts that might not be immediately apparent from quantitative data alone.
   b. This integration aids in risk mitigation, as negative sentiment is an early warning sign for stocks losing favor
   despite historical solid momentum.

This example illustrates how sentiment analysis, powered by
ChatGPT, can add a layer of depth to existing quantitative investment strategies. By combining complex data with nuanced sentiment
analysis, investment firms can achieve a more comprehensive and
balanced approach, potentially leading to more informed and strategically sound investment decisions.

Risk Management: ChatGPT for Early Warnings and Mitigating Losses

Risk management is a pivotal component in investments, ensuring
the mitigation of potential losses and the stability of investment portfolios. Incorporating AI, particularly ChatGPT, in risk management
strategies marks a significant advancement, allowing us to detect and
respond to risks more effectively and swiftly.

Risk management in investments fundamentally revolves around
identifying and mitigating factors that could lead to financial losses.
Traditional risk management approaches often rely on historical data
and standard financial metrics. However, adding AI-driven tools like
ChatGPT offers a more dynamic and proactive approach.

ChatGPT's most significant contribution to risk management is its
ability to function as an early warning system. By detecting shifts in
market sentiment, ChatGPT can identify potential risks before they
materialize into substantial financial impacts. For instance, a sudden
surge in negative sentiment around a specific sector or company,
as ChatGPT detected, could indicate an impending downturn or a
brewing crisis. This early detection is crucial in allowing investors
and fund managers to take preemptive actions, such as adjusting
their portfolios or hedging against potential losses.

Integrating ChatGPT into existing risk management frameworks
requires a strategic approach. Its insights should complement, not

replace, traditional risk assessment tools. For instance, while ChatGPT might signal a negative sentiment around a technology stock, a formal analysis involving the company's financial health and market position should also be considered before deciding to sell or hold.

Moreover, ChatGPT's real-time monitoring capability stands out as a critical feature. In financial markets, the ability to receive timely updates about changing market sentiments enables us to respond quickly to emerging risks, an essential factor in mitigating potential losses.

However, we should acknowledge the limitations of relying solely on AI for risk management. Instances of false positives or the inability of AI to capture incredibly nuanced human insights are potential pitfalls. An effective strategy involves a balanced approach, where AI-driven insights from ChatGPT are used with human expertise and traditional risk assessment methods.

EXAMPLE: ChatGPT IN RISK MANAGEMENT– DETECTING AND RESPONDING TO MARKET SHIFTS

Scenario: Consider an investment firm specializing in technology stocks. The firm relies on quantitative analysis and traditional market research to manage its investment portfolio.

Integration of ChatGPT for Risk Detection: The firm integrates ChatGPT into its risk management system to monitor and analyze market sentiments around technology stocks and the broader tech sector.

Step-by-Step Application:

1. Real-time Sentiment Analysis:
   a. ChatGPT continuously scans various data sources, including tech news websites, financial forums, and social media platforms, focusing on companies within the firm's portfolio.
   b. It analyzes the sentiment of the content, identifying trends and shifts in perceptions about these companies or the tech sector in general.
2. Detecting a Negative Sentiment Shift:
   a. ChatGPT detects a growing negative sentiment around a specific technology stock in the firm's portfolio. This sentiment

shift, triggered by critical articles and negative social media discussions about the company's latest product release, is flagged to the firm's analysts.

3. Correlating with Quantitative Data:
   a. The firm's analysts review the sentiment analysis provided by ChatGPT alongside their quantitative data, such as the stock's recent price movements, trading volume, and historical performance.

4. Making an Informed Decision:
   a. Based on the combined insights from ChatGPT and their quantitative analysis, the analysts conclude that the negative sentiment will likely adversely impact the stock's price.
   b. They decide to reduce their position in the stock, mitigating potential losses.

5. Monitoring for Further Developments:
   a. The firm continues to use ChatGPT to monitor the situation, looking for any changes in sentiment or additional information that might warrant revisiting their decision.

6. Outcome:
   a. The company's stock price dropped significantly in the following weeks, validating the decision to reduce exposure based on the early warning from ChatGPT.
   b. The firm avoids considerable losses by acting on the insights provided by the AI-driven sentiment analysis.

This example illustrates how ChatGPT can be a valuable asset in risk management within the investment sector. By providing real-time sentiment analysis, it helps in detecting potential market shifts that could affect investment performance. When combined with traditional quantitative analysis, the insights provided by ChatGPT can help us make more informed decisions and manage and mitigate risks effectively.

Integrating ChatGPT in Automated Trading Systems

Automatic trading systems employ algorithmic strategies based on statistical and mathematical models. These models traditionally rely on quantitative data such as price movements, trading volumes, and economic indicators. However, the integration of AI, and specifically ChatGPT, brings a new dimension to these systems. ChatGPT, with its advanced sentiment analysis capabilities, offers a better understanding of market dynamics by interpreting the mood and opinions reflected in news articles, social media, and financial reports.

TRADING SIGNALS AND RISK MANAGEMENT

The incorporation of ChatGPT into trading algorithms involves translating its sentiment analysis into quantitative signals that can be understood and utilized by these automated systems. This capability enables the systems to make more informed decisions, potentially leading to increased profitability and better risk-adjusted returns.

ChatGPT also plays a vital role in risk management within automated trading systems. By providing early warnings about shifts in market sentiment, ChatGPT can help preempt adverse market movements, allowing the systems to adjust their strategies accordingly. This proactive approach to risk management is invaluable in protecting investment portfolios from sudden market downturns.

ORDER TYPES AND TIMING

ChatGPT can enhance trading systems by suggesting order types and timing trades. By analyzing the prevailing sentiment in market conditions, ChatGPT can guide algorithms to select the most suitable type of order. For instance, bid-ask spreads typically widen in a highly volatile market, making market orders more dangerous as your fill may end up well outside the quoted spread. This strategic selection of order types is crucial for enhancing trade efficacy and managing risk.

Simultaneously, ChatGPT's proficiency in discerning sentiment trends enables it to predict shifts in market momentum. Understanding these trends allows ChatGPT to advise on the optimal timing for trade execution. For instance, if there is a favorable change in sentiment surrounding a particular stock, ChatGPT can signal the trading system to execute a buy order before the market reacts and prices increase. Conversely, it can suggest selling ahead of anticipated adverse movements.

ChatGPT can analyze and act on real-time sentiment trends, giving us an edge in the fast-paced trading environment. It can improve the accuracy and profitability of trade executions in automated trading systems. Customizing trading strategies is a dynamic and critical aspect of integrating ChatGPT into automated trading systems. ChatGPT can significantly contribute to strategy adjustment through the lens of current market sentiment.

For instance, if the prevailing view is bullish, it may suggest an aggressive strategy to capitalize on upward trends. Conversely, it might recommend a more defensive stance in bearish or volatile conditions, focusing on the preservation of capital and risk mitigation. This flexibility allows for responsive and tailored trading approaches that align closely with aggregate market dynamics.

Regarding portfolio diversification, ChatGPT's understanding of broader market sentiment is invaluable. It can analyze trends and sentiment across various sectors and asset classes, suggesting reallocations to mitigate risks or capture growth.

For example, ChatGPT might recommend increasing the portfolio's allocation to traditionally defensive sectors or assets in anticipation of a market downturn. Alternatively, it could recommend increasing exposure to a particular industry as it sees growth potential. By continuously monitoring and interpreting market mood, ChatGPT aids in constructing a more resilient and opportunistic investment portfolio tailored to the market landscape.

REPORTING

The potential for automated reporting by integrating ChatGPT into trading systems presents a transformative opportunity for stakeholder engagement and decision-making. This approach could generate concise summaries and reports on trading activities and market conditions.

Stakeholders could gain real-time insights into performance metrics such as profit and loss, risk exposure, and strategy adherence, which is especially valuable in rapidly changing market environments. This potential system promises a leap in transparency and continuous insight, allowing stakeholders to efficiently grasp the nuances of strategy execution, market trends, and portfolio adjustments. Automated reporting would streamline monitoring and decision-making, giving stakeholders a more strategic understanding of their investments.

In addition to data summarization, ChatGPT's potential use in automated reporting could revolutionize the interpretative aspect of financial data. Stakeholders could benefit from nuanced explanations and predictive insights to better understand market movements and trading outcomes. For instance, alongside performance metrics, the system could provide context on market sentiment shifts, emerging trends, or unforeseen events impacting the portfolio, using lay terms to clarify complex financial jargon.

Financial information could be democratized through this level of detailed and accessible reporting, making it not only more accessible but also actionable for a broader range of stakeholders, regardless of their financial expertise. As such, the potential adoption of ChatGPT in automated reporting represents a step toward more informed, proactive, and responsive investment management.

RISKS AND CHALLENGES

While the benefits of integrating ChatGPT into automated trading systems are clear, it is crucial to consider the associated risks and challenges. The reliance on AI for financial decisions raises questions about data quality, model adaptability, regulatory compliance, and the overall robustness of trading strategies.

As we integrate ChatGPT into trading systems, understanding these risks and challenges becomes essential for maintaining the integrity and efficiency of these advanced technological systems. Most of these challenges are pertinent for fine-tuned versions of ChatGPT and other advanced LLMs designed for stock trading.

Over-Reliance on AI

Integrating ChatGPT and similar AI technologies into automated trading systems has undoubtedly brought significant advancements. However, an over-reliance on these AI-driven decisions poses substantial risks.

Primarily, there is a danger that the nuanced understanding and critical thinking inherent to human traders could be overshadowed by AI's seemingly efficient and rapid analysis. While adept at processing large volumes of data and identifying patterns, algorithms still lack the qualitative judgment and ethical considerations that human oversight brings. Even advanced models can only reason a couple of steps ahead.

This reliance may be particularly concerning when AI-driven strategies are used without sufficient understanding of their underlying mechanisms or limitations, leading to decisions that might not fully account for complex market dynamics or rare, unforeseeable events. Moreover, over-reliance on AI can lead to a homogenization of trading strategies. As more traders and firms adopt similar AI models, the strategy distinctiveness diminishes, potentially leading to market inefficiencies or systemic vulnerabilities.

Furthermore, there is also the risk of feedback loops where AI-driven decisions continually reinforce and amplify specific market trends, which might not accurately reflect underlying economic realities. This concentration of similar trades can create bubbles or exacerbate market downturns.

Lastly, the potential for overlooking human insight is significant. Human traders interpret data and apply a wealth of experience, intuition, and understanding of context—particularly crucial aspects during market stress or when navigating uncharted economic conditions. LLMs may not yet have the flexibility to adapt to scenarios outside of what they have learned.

AI can enhance decision-making, but human judgment is essential for interpreting AI's recommendations and understanding its limitations. This balance mitigates the risks of over-reliance on AI, ensuring that automated trading systems are robust, adaptable, and aligned with economic considerations.

Data Quality and Interpretation Challenges

The efficacy of ChatGPT in automated trading systems depends on the quality and variety of input data it receives. The model requires access to high-quality, relevant, and diverse data sources for successful sentiment analysis, including news articles, financial reports, and social media content.

The data must be comprehensive, timely, and accurately reflect market conditions and sentiments. Data of poor quality, such as outdated, irrelevant, or biased data, can lead to inaccurate analyses and misguided trading decisions. This reliance on quality data is a critical vulnerability, as even the most advanced AI models are only as good as the data they process.

Moreover, interpreting the lack of up-to-date data presents a significant hurdle. ChatGPT and LLMs are updated with new data only a few times yearly. Models integrated into automatic systems are usually not tasked with browsing online for the latest information, even though they can. The lack of timely data can dramatically alter the sentiment and meaning of a text. It can be especially relevant when models are tasked with predicting economic outcomes.

Sophisticated NLP techniques and ongoing model training are required to improve AI's understanding of human language. These methods involve teaching models to recognize and interpret various linguistic nuances and continually updating them with new data to reflect the latest information and market trends. We can also provide up-to-date information as part of the prompt.

Despite these efforts, the inherent complexities of human language and the ever-evolving nature of communication will continue to pose significant data quality and interpretation challenges in integrating ChatGPT into automated trading systems.

Market Adaptability and Model Obsolescence

Economic policies, investor behavior, global events, and technological advancements constantly influence financial markets. This dynamic nature requires trading models, particularly those incorporating AI like ChatGPT, to be highly adaptable and responsive to new information and market conditions.

As markets evolve, model obsolescence is a significant risk. Strategies that were effective yesterday may not be tomorrow as market dynamics shift or as other market participants adapt and change their strategies. AI models need continual learning and updating to maintain relevance and effectiveness.

As the market changes, the predictions and strategies derived from AI models may diverge from reality, resulting in suboptimal or even detrimental trading decisions. To address this, AI models require robust mechanisms for continuous learning, enabling them to adapt to new data and conditions. This learning may involve retraining the model with new data, incorporating feedback loops, or using adaptive algorithms that can evolve with the market.

Continuous adaptation, though advantageous, also presents several challenges. For one thing, it requires a delicate equilibrium between responsiveness to market fluctuations and stability to avoid overfitting to short-term market noise. Additionally, it requires significant computational resources and expertise to monitor, update, and validate models. Furthermore, as models become more complex and self-adaptive, the risk of unintended consequences or behaviors increases, necessitating rigorous testing and oversight.

While adaptable AI models, like ChatGPT, are a powerful tool for trading, they also present some challenges. For example, ensuring that these models remain relevant and profitable as markets evolve is crucial. This dynamic requires ongoing effort, resources, and a careful model management and governance approach. Without this, there is a risk that the models will become obsolete, which could negatively impact trading performance. Therefore, it is vital to manage the risk of model obsolescence.

Risk of Echo Chambers and Amplification of Errors

Integrating AI like ChatGPT into automatic trading systems risks creating echo chambers and amplifying errors, two interrelated issues that can distort market perceptions and trading efficacy. Echo chambers occur when trading algorithms, operating on similar data sources and strategies, begin to reflect and reinforce prevailing market sentiments.

Sentiment analysis, in particular, is prone to this issue, as multiple trading systems may interpret and react uniformly to news or social media trends, creating a self-reinforcing cycle of market moves. This concentration contrasts with a diverse set of independent strategies operating in the market, which would lead to more varied reactions and less exaggerated movements in asset prices. In some cases, this blending of responses can even lead to market bubbles.

Additionally, including AI in trading systems can amplify the errors or biases already present in the data. AI models like ChatGPT rely on the data they are trained on and operate with. If this data contains biases, inaccuracies, or systematic errors, the AI will inherently reflect these issues in its analysis and decision-making.

For instance, if sentiment analysis tools consistently misconstrue certain kinds of news or are fed biased news sources, their trading signals may be systematically biased. This problem is compounded when many trading systems use similar or the same data sources and AI models, as the same errors are replicated and amplified across the market.

The amplification can also occur through feedback loops. As AI-driven trades influence the market, they generate new data, fed back into the same trading systems. If the initial decisions are erroneous or biased, they can be amplified and exaggerated over time, leading to increasingly distorted trading behavior and market dynamics. AI-driven trades can significantly impact market prices and trends, posing a risk in fast-moving or illiquid markets.

A false trend can quickly snowball into a significant market distortion through feedback loops in a market dominated by AI-driven trading systems. For example, consider a scenario where these systems, analyzing mixed sentiments about a tech company's rumored product launch, mistakenly interpret fake articles as positive signals.

As some AIs begin buying up the company's stock based on these misinterpretations, the price rises, misleading other automated systems into believing there is a genuine bullish trend. These purchases create a self-reinforcing cycle: the price increase, driven by AI purchases, validates the initial misinterpretation, leading to further buying and a continued rise in the stock price.

However, when the actual product is revealed to be less impactful than the market has been led to believe, the inflated stock price corrects sharply, causing a rapid downturn. Those who are late in reacting incur substantial losses.

This scenario exemplifies the risks inherent in feedback loops where initial AI errors get amplified through market reactions, leading to overinflated asset values. It highlights the need for robust error detection and correction mechanisms in AI systems and emphasizes the importance of maintaining human oversight to mitigate the effects of such distortions in fast-moving or illiquid markets.

In addressing these challenges, developers and users of AI trading systems must ensure diversity in strategies and data sources, apply rigorous testing and validation of models, and maintain a level of human oversight and intervention.

In addition, comprehending and mitigating these risks entails ongoing surveillance for indications of echo chamber effects or error amplification, along with adaptable techniques that can react to and rectify such problems. The risk of echo chambers and error amplification can destabilize and corrupt financial markets without careful management, converting the tools to improve trading efficiency into catalysts for market distortion.

Unpredictable Market Behavior and Black Swan Events
Integrating AI, including tools like ChatGPT, in automated trading systems introduces specific vulnerabilities to unpredictable market behavior and extreme Black Swan events. These are rare, unexpected events that are severe and sometimes evident in hindsight.

AI models, even ChatGPT and those fine-tuned in trading strategies, are typically trained on historical data and thus are inherently limited to learning from what has already happened. They excel in stable or slowly evolving environments where past patterns indicate future trends. However, they may struggle to anticipate or react appropriately to novel scenarios that diverge significantly from historical precedents.

Unprecedented market conditions, such as a sudden economic crisis, geopolitical conflict, or a global pandemic, can cause rapid and unpredictable market sentiment and behavior changes. In such situations, the predictive power of AI models can decrease as the patterns and relationships they have learned become less relevant. The models may produce inaccurate predictions, be unable to adapt quickly to new market conditions, or overlook subtle cues that a human trader may notice.

In addition to the inability to predict Black Swan events, AI-driven trading poses the risk of unforeseen or unintended system responses to the extreme market volatility and rare conditions that accompany such events. For instance, AI systems may excessively buy or sell assets, amplify market movements, or behave in a coordinated manner, resulting in a cascade of trades that exacerbate market shocks.

Furthermore, the lack of historical data for these rare and unpredictable events means that AI systems, including ChatGPT, have limited reference points for learning how to handle such situations. Despite sophisticated modeling techniques and attempts to simulate extreme conditions, the inherent uncertainty and variability of Black Swan events make them a persistent challenge for AI in trading systems.

To reduce these risks, it is vital for automated trading systems to use effective risk management techniques, have a degree of human oversight, and ensure that AI models are as flexible and robust as possible. Furthermore, traders and firms must be aware of AI's limitations in dealing with unpredictable market behavior and ensure that their systems can promptly revert to human control when required.

Despite the advancements in AI, the unpredictable nature of financial markets and the occurrence of Black Swan events remain significant challenges that require careful consideration and planning in integrating AI into automated trading systems.

As financial institutions increasingly use AI for automated trading, it is crucial to take a balanced approach. AI offers substantial benefits, such as enhanced data analysis and improved decision-making speed. However, some significant risks and challenges must be carefully managed. A balanced approach requires acknowledging the innovative potential of AI while being aware of the limitations and risks associated with over-reliance, data quality, market adaptability, echo chambers, and the handling of unpredictable market conditions and Black Swan events.

It is vital to harness the strengths of AI to complement human expertise, not replace it. Human oversight remains crucial in interpreting AI analysis, providing qualitative insights, and stepping in during extreme market conditions. Financial firms must invest in robust infrastructure, ongoing model training and updating, and rigorous testing and validation to guarantee that AI systems are as accurate, adaptable, and secure as possible. Strategies and models must be regularly evaluated and refined in response to new data and changing market conditions, promoting continuous learning and adaptability.

Regulatory considerations and ethical implications of automated trading also demand attention, ensuring that the integration of AI into financial markets contributes to their stability and integrity. Regulators, industry peers, and other stakeholders must work closely to establish standards and best practices for AI in trading.

Integrating ChatGPT into automated trading systems represents a significant stride toward more sophisticated and informed trading strategies. By merging the power of AI-driven sentiment analysis with algorithmic trading, these systems are becoming more efficient and better at navigating financial markets. The way ahead is to adopt AI in automated trading systems while staying mindful of its complexities and challenges.

ChatGPT's role in the financial sector represents a paradigm shift, particularly in how market analysis and investment decisions are approached. Through sentiment analysis, integration in investment strategies, risk management, and automated trading systems, we have seen the multifaceted impact of ChatGPT in finance.

Summary

In this chapter, we discovered the diverse applications ChatGPT has in financial forecasting and trading, ranging from enhancing investment strategies to optimizing automated trading systems. Specifically, we grasped how integrating sentiment analysis from ChatGPT can improve traditional and quantitative investing approaches by providing additional insights into market perceptions.

Additionally, we understood how ChatGPT serves as an early warning system for risk management by detecting shifts in market sentiment before changes are reflected elsewhere. This capability enables preemptive actions to mitigate potential losses.

ChatGPT can optimize elements like order timing, risk controls, and stakeholder reporting when incorporated into automated trading systems. However, the chapter emphasized the importance of balancing automation with human oversight to check on over-reliance on AI and ensure system resilience to unpredictable events.

We also became aware of multiple risks accompanying the integration of AI, like ChatGPT, into complex trading systems. These include challenges tied to model accuracy, echo chambers, error amplification, and adaptability to evolving markets over time. Internalizing these limitations is central to managing the risks when applying AI tools.

Overall, this chapter gave us perspective on ChatGPT's innovative use cases for financial analysis and trading. We understood the need to embrace the possibilities of AI while cultivating human expertise, honing model adaptability and proactively addressing risks inherent in these advanced systems. The future landscape will likely see AI play an increasingly prominent role.

Coming Up Next

The next chapter will investigate AI technology advancements and how they shape the financial industry. From the development of more sophisticated machine learning models to the integration of AI in various aspects of financial services, this section will provide a glimpse into the cutting-edge technologies that are set to redefine financial forecasting and trading.

The chapter will also explore future research directions, discussing the potential avenues for innovation and exploration in AI-driven financial strategies. This section aims to highlight the areas where research is most fervently needed, exploring how advancements in AI could address current limitations and open new opportunities for financial forecasting and analysis.

Expect a chapter brimming with insights on the evolving landscape of AI in finance, packed with expert opinions, case studies, and projections about where the field is headed. Whether you have years of experience in finance, a deep interest in AI, or simply a curiosity about the future of technology and finance, this chapter will provide valuable perspectives and provoke thought about the endless possibilities that AI holds for the world of financial forecasting.

Check Your Understanding Questions

1. How does ChatGPT enhance traditional investment strategies with its sentiment analysis capabilities?
2. Describe how risk management benefits from integrating ChatGPT's predictive capabilities.
3. Explain the role of ChatGPT in automated trading systems and how it affects decision-making.
4. What steps are involved in combining sentiment analysis with a quantitative momentum strategy?
5. Identify the challenges and limitations of relying solely on AI for investment risk management.
6. Detail how real-time sentiment analysis by ChatGPT can lead to proactive risk mitigation.
7. Discuss the importance of balancing AI insights with traditional investment risk-assessment methods.

PART III

Envisioning a Financial Future with AI

CHAPTER 9

The Future of AI in Financial Forecasting

In finance, the emergence of AI has marked a transformative era in forecasting and decision-making. This chapter explores the potential future landscape of AI in finance. We explore how AI is poised to redefine the norms of financial analysis and investment strategies.

The objectives of this chapter are multifold. First, we highlight the most significant upcoming AI technology trends. We examine emerging algorithms, the fusion of AI with blockchain and the internet of things (IoT), and the progress in data-processing capabilities. Second, we will explore the personalization of financial services through AI, envisioning a future where financial advice and strategies are as unique as the individual investor's profile.

Furthermore, we will learn about the regulatory and ethical terrain accompanying AI integration in finance. We address the regulatory landscape, ethical considerations, and the paramount issue of data privacy in AI-driven financial practices.

Lastly, we discuss the limitations of current AI technologies in financial forecasting and AI's expected influence on the finance industry's structure. This impact includes its effect on employment, the emergence of new financial entities, and new user interfaces.

By the end of this chapter, you will have a comprehensive understanding of AI's dynamic and promising future in financial forecasting.

Emerging AI Algorithms and Models

Recently, sophisticated AI algorithms and models have accelerated, promising to revolutionize how we understand and analyze financial markets. These advancements include deep learning, reinforcement learning, neural network architectures tailored explicitly for financial applications, and LLMs.

Deep learning has remarkable pattern recognition and predictive modeling capabilities. Its capacity to handle and glean insights from extensive datasets makes it well-suited for financial forecasting. For instance, deep-learning algorithms can analyze market trends, consumer behavior, and economic indicators to predict stock price movements with increasing accuracy.

AUTOMATIC TRADING AGENTS

A promising area of deep learning is reinforcement learning (RL), which involves algorithms that learn the best course of action through trial and error. In financial contexts, algorithms would be deployed in the stock market with an initial amount of money. They should quickly adapt their trading strategies, learning from market dynamics to optimize returns.

These algorithms promise a systematic way to solve the issue of a changing world. Most AI and machine-learning methods must be constantly retrained because the world changes and their training data becomes obsolete. RL agents, in theory, can adapt to new sources of information, with the advantage that they can trade and interact automatically. Combining RL with ChatGPT and other LLMs is a promising area.

The critical advantage of RL is that agents learn optimal behaviors directly from experience and rewards without requiring large labeled datasets. An RL trader could directly interact with markets, adjusting its strategy based on what actions lead to profits or losses. This adaptable learning process seems well-suited to fast-changing financial environments.

However, markets present risks and dynamics that can negatively reinforce behaviors, confusing RL algorithms. Trading fees, bid-ask spreads, and non-stationarities like crises all complicate learning. Financial rewards are also sparse and delayed relative to the tight action loops these algorithms are designed for. An RL trader needs appropriate constraints, shaped rewards, and uncertainty modeling to explore safely.

ChatGPT integration can enhance reinforcement learning (RL) for financial applications. It could provide four essential functions: knowledge infusion, explainability, interactive reward setting, and simulation-based training.

First, ChatGPT contains substantial financial knowledge from human datasets. RL agents could query this knowledge to improve their initial trading strategies before further learning. With this knowledge, the model can be nudged toward trying profitable plans.

A key challenge in RL is directing agents to explore strategies that are likely to be profitable rather than testing every possibility without direction. However, defining a solid initial policy requires substantial expertise. For trading, that means understanding historical market behaviors, stylized facts, indicators, common strategies across assets, and theories around market microstructure. This contextual knowledge helps constrain and direct profit-seeking exploration.

ChatGPT contains broad financial knowledge from trading books, equity research, analysis reports, academic papers, and practitioner forums. This knowledge represents substantial aggregated human wisdom around markets. A reinforcement-learning agent designed for trading could query ChatGPT to obtain initial strategies and behavior constraints, which would serve as helpful priors. For example, it could receive information on trading approaches for growth stocks, typical support/resistance levels for indexes, or interpreting overnight news and events.

The financial expertise provided by ChatGPT would help RL exploration start closer to realistic, profitable strategies, avoiding bad decisions humans would not make in practice. This better starting point could help channel the open-ended learning capacity of RL toward finer optimizations with less real-world risk during initial training. ChatGPT could first translate trading strategies into code and then into numeric functions that an RL agent can directly utilize as a starting point that aligns well with how these algorithms operate.

Over time, as the system gains more experience, it can rely less on mimicking ChatGPT and form its market hypotheses and behaviors. Still, the initial foundation helps shortcut the learning curve considerably. Moreover, the RL model may query ChatGPT to understand current information.

Second, ChatGPT's conversational capabilities can provide helpful explanations of an RL trading agent's behavior, clarifying the rationale behind its actions to support robust oversight. As the RL agent interacts with real-world or simulated trading environments, it dynamically discovers and improves trading methods to maximize profitability. Although these emergent behaviors can be beneficial, they may not always align with human expectations or risk tolerances, especially in edge cases.

To audit effectively, we want to understand why the system made specific choices: What market conditions, signals, or indicators triggered a trade? How do current positions align with the agent's internal price forecasts or volatility models? Can the agent explain in words why a strategy has shifted recently?

ChatGPT's language modeling capabilities could allow users to request explanations. ChatGPT could analyze the trading logs and strategies of the RL agent, and ChatGPT could translate them into words, graphs, or conversational Q&A, all tailored to be understood by humans. Providing full accountability empowers risk monitoring. If behaviors stray into dangerous areas, such as taking on too much risk or engaging in aggressive trading, overseers can adjust rewards or constraints. With explainability, it becomes easier to correct an opaque system.

Third, humans could use dialogue to dynamically adjust reward formulations and risk limits as the RL agent trains. For example, it would be easy to say to the model, "You are taking too much risk," just as an investor would say to a risky trader. ChatGPT would then translate these instructions into actionable code, thus modifying the agent's rewards and constraints to reduce risk-taking.

Specifically, ChatGPT could alter the relative balance of rewards for profits versus penalties for losses and volatility to make the agent more conservative. It could tighten position limits, maximum drawdowns, or liquidity requirements through reward shaping. Direct natural language feedback allows rapid iteration to align the agent with changing risk-tolerances over time.

Additionally, if the human identifies specific problematic trades, they can provide this feedback through conversation to overrule and prevent the recurrence of these cases. ChatGPT would remember these problem cases, derive the patterns that led to failure, and encode constraints to avoid repeating those mistakes. This ability for evaluative feedback and rapid policy updating via dialogue is a key advantage of using language models for oversight.

Finally, ChatGPT can provide simulated economic situations, similar to how it creates images based on descriptions. RL can train in these comprehensive financial simulators without the danger of real-world hazards. With the help of large language models, the simulations can incorporate human knowledge into the learning environment.

ChatGPT can codify these economic simulations as parametric functions that generate synthetic time series data incorporating different market regimes, cycles, shocks, and structural changes. ChatGPT would provide the narratives and quantitative details behind economic scenarios to embed into these simulations. The key benefit is that the RL agent can experience various credible, human-grounded situations with reliable cause-and-effect dynamics. This powers the learning process before applying strategies in the real world.

MAKING LARGE LANGUAGE MODELS FINANCIAL EXPERTS

Large language models are impressive technologies that alter the boundaries of what is possible in prediction and understanding. However, their training is not specialized to prioritize financial tasks. LLMs trained to understand the stock market will likely result in a competitive advantage. Models that combine their contextual understanding with supervised machine learning methods promise enhanced forecasting capabilities.

As large language models grow more capable, fine-tuning them on financial text and data provides a decent starting point. However, genuinely matching human-level financial reasoning requires architectures directly shaped for markets. Rather than expecting general models to adapt, we must design integrated systems around the intricacies of finance.

Creating specialized financial AI could demand blending complementary modeling paradigms. First, transformer networks trained on financial text data could establish linguistic market understanding. They could learn contextual relationships between market drivers by preprocessing earnings call transcripts, news articles, analyst reports, and more. Fine-tuning could then calibrate them for accurate time-series forecasting of prices, volatility, and indicators. Attention mechanisms could also emphasize the most relevant forward-looking insights within documents.

However, more than text alone may be required—structured knowledge likely matters, too. Incorporating knowledge graphs encoding conceptual connections between market regimes, asset classes, and macroeconomic dependencies could make models more robust. Adding recurrent neural networks could handle temporal dynamics. Unifying these capabilities, hybrid architectures could combine the strengths of transformers, graphs, and RNNs or LSTMs. This layered modeling could mirror real-world complexity—integrating unstructured narratives, networked knowledge, and sequential trends as humans do. Rather than over-reliance on single methods, architecting integrated systems could unlock new levels of understanding.

In the future, these custom neural network architectures for finance could be a competitive advantage. These specialized networks will be designed to handle the nuances and complexities of financial data, providing more tailored and accurate forecasting models.

INTEGRATION WITH BLOCKCHAIN AND IoT

Integrating AI with technologies like blockchain and the internet of things (IoT) could create synergies that redefine financial forecasting.

Renowned for its security and transparency, blockchain technology can offer AI algorithms a reliable and tamper-proof data source. In financial forecasting, blockchain can ensure the integrity of the data used for making predictions, such as real-time transaction records. This integration can lead to more accurate and trustworthy AI-driven forecasts.

On the other hand, IoT offers a wealth of real-time data that can be invaluable for financial forecasting. IoT devices collect data ranging from consumer behavior to supply chain logistics, providing a holistic view of various financial market factors. AI algorithms can scrutinize this data and discern patterns and trends that would be impossible to detect manually.

The convergence of AI, blockchain, and IoT heralds a future where financial insights are not only derived from traditional market data but also from a broader spectrum of interconnected data sources. This integration promises enhanced accuracy, speed, and depth in financial forecasting, equipping us and analysts with the tools to make more informed decisions.

The advancements in AI technologies and their integration with other revolutionary technologies pave the way for a new frontier in financial forecasting. These developments promise to bring more accuracy, efficiency, and breadth to financial decision-making, heralding a future where AI is an indispensable tool in the finance industry.

New Sources of Data

Processing new and diverse datasets is central in finance. The future of prediction involves a more comprehensive incorporation of data sources. AI models can already analyze different data types, from structured data such as financial statements to unstructured data like news headlines and social media posts. Combining information contained in text, audio, images, and video will provide a predictive edge. Recent efforts have focused on adapting LLMs to support multimodal applications, and they should continue with new architectures that blend predictive approaches with LLMs.

LLMs are equipped to unlock value from multimodal data sources often overlooked in traditional machine-learning financial models. "Multimodal" refers to data that encompasses diverse formats like text, images, video, audio, and numerical data. Some of the potential data to use are:

- ◆ Satellite Imagery
    - Where ML models struggle to represent visual data, LLMs can correlate high-resolution imagery tracking shipping traffic, crop yields, and facility activity with economic indicators.
- ◆ Earnings Calls
    - Joint audio, video, and text analysis of earnings call briefings allows LLMs to better estimate management sentiment and linguistic cues that influence markets.
- ◆ News Narratives
    - Text combined with images, video clips, and metadata from financial news provides multidimensional representations of market narratives and investor psychology that are difficult to capture with statistics.

- ◆ Web Traffic and Engagement
  - ● Analysis of pageviews, scroll depth, social engagement, and links between finance sites measures retail sentiment and interest.
- ◆ Expert Annotations
  - ● Labels, explanations, and conversations from practitioners provide context for grounding model reasoning in financial concepts rather than simplistic statistical correlations.

LLMs can learn complex ideas and multimodal cues in these datasets through pretraining, similar to how humans learn. This multimodal ability can advance financial AI beyond surface-level statistical patterns, which are often fragile.

Personalization

Using new datasets and architectures may enhance AI's capability to tailor services to individual needs, like customized financial advice and strategies, catering to each investor's unique needs and goals. This evolution in data processing and personalization can reshape the relationship between financial service providers and their clients, making it more dynamic, responsive, and aligned with individual preferences.

AI's ability to analyze individual investor profiles, market conditions, and investment opportunities allows for the creation of tailored financial advice and strategies. Personalization in financial services means going beyond one-size-fits-all advice. AI can consider an individual's financial goals, risk tolerance, investment preferences, and historical performance to offer customized investment recommendations. This approach doesn't just increase customer satisfaction; it's also a catalyst for optimizing investment outcomes.

Additionally, AI-driven personalization extends to portfolio management. AI models can monitor and rebalance portfolios in real time, adjusting to market changes and aligning with the investor's objectives. This proactive management ensures that portfolios remain optimized under varying market conditions.

The future of financial services lies in this personalized approach, where AI interprets market data and aligns its insights with individual investor needs. This shift promises to make financial advice more accessible, accurate, and aligned with personal financial goals.

AI Regulatory and Implementation Challenges

AI offers considerable potential to transform financial services, but deploying these technologies poses significant ethical, regulatory, and practical challenges. There are issues regarding data quality and privacy, algorithmic transparency, accountability, preventing discriminatory biases, and maintaining market stability.

AI models rely heavily on comprehensive, accurate data to generate sound predictions and decisions. However, obtaining high-quality training data can be difficult, especially in emerging markets or new financial products. This can also be problematic because the financial sector deals with highly sensitive personal and business data. Inadequate, biased, or breached data can undermine predictions, violate privacy, and erode trust in AI.

Encryption, secure data storage, and transparent usage policies aligned with regulations are fundamental to using data well. With quality data and strong privacy protections, AI can use information to effectively meet compliance and reporting requirements while avoiding compromised security or algorithmic bias.

Another major challenge facing the application of AI in finance is the lack of model transparency and explainability. These AI systems' inherent "black box" opacity makes it difficult to understand how they arrive at predictions, decisions, and recommendations. Regulators are particularly concerned about using black-box AI models for functions needing high explainability—like credit scoring, loan adjudication, or risk assessment. Initiatives to enhance AI model documentation, auditing, and accessibility into factors influencing decisions can help address these pressing challenges.

As AI grows more pervasive, it poses systemic risks from potential manipulation or self-reinforcing feedback loops that can amplify volatility. While AI can skillfully analyze data, it can struggle to adapt models to sudden or unpredictable changes. Regulators can explore measures to preserve market stability amidst the rise of AI in automated trading and investment strategies.

Unforeseen market shifts could trigger faulty AI-driven decisions and trades that destabilize markets. To counteract this risk, regulatory bodies should develop oversight mechanisms to monitor AI trading patterns and manage vulnerabilities that could negatively impact broader stability and trust. Researchers can also improve model agility by combining AI with machine learning techniques to better detect and adapt to emerging market shifts.

Future improvements in data processing capabilities and the development of more robust data collection methods would enhance data quality, and advances in AI interpretability and explainability could make these systems more transparent and trustworthy. Efforts to identify and mitigate algorithmic bias should be underway, with researchers developing more equitable and ethical AI models. Additionally, integrating AI with other technologies could improve its adaptability and responsiveness to market changes.

AI's Potential Effects on the Financial Industry

The influence of AI on the financial industry will be significant, transforming jobs and the industry structure and creating new financial firms.

AI may automate many routine tasks in finance, leading to job displacement in some areas and creating new opportunities in others. Roles involving data analysis, risk assessment, and customer service will likely see significant automation. However, this shift could also create demand for professionals skilled in AI, data science, and machine learning and those who can interpret and apply AI-driven insights.

Moreover, AI could help democratize financial services, making sophisticated analysis and tools accessible to smaller firms and individual investors. This democratization would likely challenge traditional financial institutions and spur the growth of fintech startups and digital-only banks. The industry is moving toward more personalized, efficient, and automated services, reshaping its traditional structure. AI is already creating new financial entities, such as AI-driven investment funds, robo-advisors, and decentralized finance (DeFi) platforms. These entities offer services that were not possible before the advent of AI, changing the landscape of investment and personal finance. These trends are likely to continue.

Development of Interactive AI Interfaces

Intuitive, interactive interfaces are imperative for driving the mass adoption of AI in financial services. As conversational assistants and chatbots become ubiquitous in everyday consumer technology, AI interfaces for financial professionals and retail investors should increasingly adopt natural language interactions. Financial service providers developing AI capabilities can look to the promise of intuitive voice control and text-based chat emerging in platforms from smart speakers to messaging apps. Approachable interfaces would lower the expertise required to benefit from data-driven insights and recommendations. Interface customizability also promotes sticky usage by allowing personalization of the interaction.

Enhanced interactivity, like natural language processing capabilities, will enable users to interact with AI tools more conversationally and responsively. Users could ask questions, request specific analyses, or seek investment advice in real time. For example, a retail investor in the future could have a dialogue with a robo-advisor chatbot, asking about options to adjust their retirement portfolio after a job change. The AI assistant would understand the query contextually, rapidly analyze the user's profile and accounts, and then explain personalized recommendations to increase savings rates, shift fund allocations, and enroll in a new employer-sponsored plan. It would allow users to customize alerts for regular portfolio check-ins, projections based on various market conditions, and other tailored analytics. Effortlessly conversing with an intelligent system integrated with the user's financial data platforms would enable more informed, tailored participation and advice for everyday investors.

Summary

In this chapter, we explored the future landscape of AI in financial forecasting. We learned about upcoming AI trends like deep learning, reinforcement learning, and the fusion of AI with blockchain and IoT. These advancements promise to bring more accuracy, efficiency, and breadth to financial decision-making, heralding a future where AI is an indispensable tool in finance.

However, deploying AI poses significant ethical and regulatory challenges. These include issues around data privacy, algorithmic transparency and accountability, preventing biases, and maintaining market stability. We learned that initiatives around data encryption, model interpretability, identifying bias, and oversight for systemic risks could enable AI's safe, fair, and effective integration in finance.

The influence of AI on the finance industry itself will be transformative. We learned how it could reshape jobs and create new types of firms like AI-driven investment funds and robo-advisors. This could democratize access to sophisticated tools while challenging traditional institutions. The changes may also include a rising demand for talent skilled in emerging technologies like AI and machine learning.

Intuitive, interactive interfaces will be imperative for driving the mass adoption of AI in finance, as we studied. Approaches like voice control, chatbots, and customizability will make these tools more accessible to professionals and everyday investors. More responsiveness enabled by natural language processing could also let users get tailored financial advice and easily adjust recommendations to their needs.

Coming Up Next
The concluding chapter combines the insights and knowledge gained throughout the book. We begin with a brief overview of our journey, revisiting the pivotal role of AI in the current financial context. The chapter will summarize the core concepts covered in the book, from the evolution of AI in business to the specific impact of models like ChatGPT on financial forecasting. The concluding chapter will inspire you about AI's transformative potential in finance and encourage active engagement and continuous innovation. As we finish, you will find yourself equipped with a deep understanding of AI's role in finance, ready to shape the future of financial decision-making.

Check Your Understanding Questions
◆ Advancements in AI Technologies: What are some emerging AI algorithms and models that are likely to impact financial forecasting? Discuss how these advancements differ from traditional financial analysis methods.

◆ Integration of AI with Blockchain and IoT: Explain how integrating AI with technologies like blockchain and the internet of things (IoT) can enhance financial forecasting. Provide examples of potential applications of this integration.

◆ Data Processing and Personalization in AI: How does AI contribute to efficiency in data analysis in finance? Discuss the potential of AI in offering personalized financial services and the implications for investors.

◆ Navigating the Regulatory Landscape: Identify and discuss the key regulatory challenges associated with AI in financial forecasting. How do these challenges impact the implementation and trustworthiness of AI in financial decision-making?

◆ Ethical Considerations and Data Privacy: What are the primary ethical dilemmas and data privacy concerns surrounding the use of AI in finance? What measures can be taken to tackle these concerns and ensure the ethical use of AI applications?

◆ Overcoming AI Limitations: What are the current limitations of AI in financial forecasting, and how might future developments address these limitations? Discuss the importance of adaptability in AI models to changing market conditions.

◆ AI's Influence on the Financial Industry: Predict how AI might impact the structure of the financial industry, focusing on aspects such as employment, industry dynamics, and the emergence of new financial entities.

◆ Investor Education and AI Literacy: Why is investor education and AI literacy decisive in AI-driven financial forecasting? How can enhanced AI literacy benefit individual investors and the broader financial community?

◆ Development of Interactive AI Interfaces: Describe the future advancements you envision in user-friendly AI tools for finance. How can these advancements improve user engagement and the overall utility of AI in financial decision-making?

CHAPTER 10

How AI Is Shaping Our Economic Future

Throughout this book, we have explored artificial intelligence and finance's fascinating and rapidly evolving intersection. We began our journey by exploring the fundamentals of artificial intelligence, mainly focusing on large language models like ChatGPT. Our exploration took us through machine learning and AI, highlighting how these technologies have revolutionized how we approach complex problems, including financial forecasting.

We learned the methodologies of stock market predictions, contrasting traditional approaches with the groundbreaking potential offered by AI and machine learning. Then, we shifted our focus to an in-depth analysis of ChatGPT, examining its capabilities, the power of its prompts, and its practical applications in the business world. We also discussed ethical considerations surrounding using such technology in sensitive areas like finance.

In subsequent chapters, we followed a detailed study on ChatGPT's potential to forecast stock price movements and a practical guide on designing and implementing AI-driven trading strategies. We also explored other specific applications in risk management and speculated about how the future models will reshape the landscape. In this journey, we acquired insights into the capabilities of current AI models and their practical applications in real-world financial decision-making.

In this book's conclusion, we will begin by summarizing our learning journey, emphasizing the core insights and knowledge you acquired, and reflecting on the practical takeaways. Then, we will explore AI's potential future developments. Finally, we will learn how to continue participating in the ongoing conversation about AI and stay updated on the latest developments.

What We Learned

The book's chapters demonstrated AI's disruptive influence and potential for future financial innovations. The following sections will provide a concise summary of our journey, examine potential applications, explore ethical concerns, and look ahead to the future of AI in finance, consolidating the knowledge and insights gained throughout this book.

UNDERSTANDING THE STOCK MARKET

We first explored the fundamental concepts and mechanics of the stock market. We learned about the economic functions of markets in enabling trading, raising capital, allocating resources, and gauging economic health. We covered the basics of trading stocks, including how they represent ownership, different order types, market participants like brokers and regulators, and fundamental and technical analysis techniques to inform decisions.

We also learned about effective portfolio management. We studied passive investing, value, growth, and income investing strategies to align investments to financial goals. We also studied risk management techniques like diversification and asset allocation. Finally, we explored fundamental terms like returns, alpha, beta, volatility, and the Sharpe ratio to evaluate investment performance and risk.

UNDERSTANDING ARTIFICIAL INTELLIGENCE

This chapter introduced artificial intelligence, laying the conceptual groundwork to explore its financial applications. We learned about the components of AI systems, including hardware, software, algorithms, and neural networks that enable machines to perform human-like cognitive functions. The chapter covered different machine learning models—supervised, unsupervised, and reinforcement learning— that allow computers to gain intelligence from data patterns.

Additionally, we studied AI's capabilities and limitations, compared to human cognition, and the history and evolution of AI approaches leading up to today's deep learning techniques. Modern neural networks have enabled breakthroughs like computer vision and natural language processing. As these technologies continue rapidly advancing, AI is poised to transform many aspects of finance, from sentiment analysis for algorithmic trading to automated financial advising. Grasping these AI foundations provides the context to understand its emerging use cases.

LARGE LANGUAGE MODELS: A GAME CHANGER

This chapter explored how large language models (LLMs) are advancing natural language processing (NLP) and generative AI capabilities to new frontiers. We learned how LLMs like GPT-3 can analyze text data like earnings reports and generate personalized investment recommendations. We overviewed NLP techniques like named entity recognition, sentiment analysis, text summarization, and machine translation that enable practical financial applications.

We also studied the mechanics of generative AI models, including their vast data ingestion and statistical learning that allows coherent creative generation. This set the context for introducing LLMs and transformer architectures, enabling them to interpret text with unparalleled context and parameter scale. However, we also discussed problems like biases that need solving before LLMs' potential is fully realized. Overall, this chapter laid the groundwork for leveraging these state-of-the-art natural language models to develop trading strategies while accounting for their limitations. It showcased LLMs' immense promise to enhance decision-making through language understanding and generation.

ADVANCED TOPICS IN LLMs

Here, we explored the advanced architectures that empower large language models to achieve unprecedented natural language understanding and generation capabilities. We learned about transformers and self-attention, which allow models to interpret textual context and identify relevant connections. Additional architectures like encoder-decoder models are ideal for tasks ranging from classification to translation.

We also studied methods for enhancing large language models through transfer learning, which adapts pre-trained models to new tasks and fine-tuning on domain-specific data. Adjusting model specifications can balance creative freedom and output accuracy. Prominent models like GPT-4 and Claude showcase diverse state-of-the-art capabilities and limitations, contributing to rapid innovation in natural language AI. As these models evolve, priorities include improving efficiency, ethics, and versatility while enabling smooth application integration. These architectures and enhancement strategies underscore how large language models achieve remarkable language understanding, creation, and problem-solving.

WHAT IS CHATGPT?

We then thoroughly studied ChatGPT's advanced natural language processing capabilities powered by deep learning. We learned how ChatGPT can analyze text input and generate remarkably human-like responses by leveraging foundations like large language models and generative AI. These technologies enable ChatGPT to engage in contextual conversations, follow instructions, execute code, and more.

However, we also covered ChatGPT's limitations, including lack of understanding, short-term memory, sensitivity to prompts, and risk of biases or mistakes. We learned techniques to mitigate these issues, like decomposing complex goals and engineering effective prompts to guide the model. Additionally, we surveyed valuable real-world applications of ChatGPT in areas like content creation and customer service while noting persisting ethical challenges around data privacy, bias, and transparency that necessitate human oversight.

CAN CHATGPT FORECAST STOCK PRICE MOVEMENTS?

This chapter explored the research conducted with my coauthor, Yuehua Tang, on whether advanced natural language models like ChatGPT could forecast stock returns by analyzing news headlines. We learned how the study assembled stock prices, headlines, and sentiment scores to train and test ChatGPT's predictive capabilities. ChatGPT significantly outperformed baseline models, with trading strategies informed by its sentiment analysis of news yielding market-beating returns. Its short recommendations for stocks with negative sentiment were highly effective, although a combined long-short approach works better. Newer models like GPT-4 also showed superior sophistication in interpreting complex news.

These findings have profound implications for transforming financial analysis and strategies through AI while raising ethical considerations. As advanced language models continue rapidly evolving in performance and capabilities, integrating them into finance necessitates developing rigorous frameworks to ensure optimal outcomes.

Practical Lessons

ChatGPT's ability to understand, process, and generate human-like text opens new possibilities for analyzing financial markets. One of the most significant impacts of ChatGPT in financial forecasting is its ability to perform sentiment analysis on a large scale. By analyzing news headlines, social media posts, and financial reports, ChatGPT can quantify market sentiment, which is a vital indicator of stock market movements.

The study shows how to exploit this capability to make better-informed decisions grounded in market trends and investor sentiments. We can use these insights to manage and mitigate risks, reduce the likelihood of substantial losses, and enhance our investment portfolios. Furthermore, ChatGPT can process information in multiple languages, providing insights into international markets and enabling a more holistic approach to global investment strategies.

One of the critical advantages of LLMs is their potential for customization. These models can be tailored to analyze and predict trends within sectors, regions, or data types. Training ChatGPT, or other LLMs, on targeted datasets can make its forecasts highly specialized and relevant to specific investment strategies or market considerations. Whether focusing on a global market, a niche industry, or types of financial instruments, ChatGPT's flexible architecture can be adapted to meet diverse analytical needs.

AI and machine learning models constantly evolve, with new architectures continually being developed. Hence, we need to stay up to date on the latest advances and understand how these tools are changing so that we can use them efficiently. Continuous engagement with AI models is indispensable for developing, refining, and adapting investment strategies. We must proactively learn and incorporate new insights analogous to how AI models evolve and improve.

Implications

AI systems will transform the roles of financial analysts, who may spend less time on manual work and more on gathering data or implementing models. Investment strategies across firms will shift to be more data-driven, relying on insights from language models to gain a competitive edge. There may be rising demand for specialized roles in model oversight, refinement, and ensuring ethical use.

Advanced predictive models could promote inclusivity for retail investors by making sophisticated analysis more accessible. However, better financial education about using these tools responsibly will be crucial. As trades increasingly stem from model recommendations, transparency and accountability around AI systems will be critical, underscoring the need for explainable reasoning.

Advanced language models could help governments better predict economic shifts, provide personalized financial advice tailored to individual risk profiles, and bring sophisticated tools even to emerging markets. However, appropriate regulation and collaboration between finance and tech remain instrumental in directing these technologies to benefit society broadly.

The study's findings represent a breakthrough in financial forecasting. They demonstrate the practical utility of AI models like ChatGPT in stock market analysis and open new avenues for exploration and innovation in finance. These insights will continue to shape how financial markets are analyzed.

IMPLEMENTING A ChatGPT TRADING STRATEGY: A STEP-BY-STEP GUIDE

This chapter taught us how to build a ChatGPT-driven trading strategy successfully. Developing a ChatGPT-driven trading strategy begins with understanding AI capabilities in sentiment analysis. ChatGPT can analyze vast amounts of news and extract trading signals by identifying market sentiment shifts.

Practical Lessons

The initial phase of deploying AI tools in finance involves assessing investment goals and risk tolerance to ensure alignment with our investment objectives and risk appetite. We can then use LLMs and AI to identify potentially profitable signals.

After identifying these signals, practical strategy development emphasizes disciplined position sizing and a mean-variance optimization framework to manage risk. Rigorous backtesting against historical data evaluates the strategy's viability across various market conditions, highlighting any weaknesses that need addressing before real-world implementation. We must also prioritize establishing robust data management systems to guarantee up-to-date information and high-quality data sources.

Once the strategy passes the testing phase, trade execution can be automated with integrated risk management practices to ensure market dynamics resilience. However, sustainable success requires constant vigilance—the strategy must be monitored and adaptively adjusted as market sentiment and conditions inevitably shift over time. Key considerations include being aware of potential regulatory requirements.

Strategies in finance are not static; they require ongoing monitoring and adaptation to maintain their effectiveness. A continuous monitoring, evaluation, and adaptation cycle can help strategies remain competitive.

Implications

Markets are increasingly efficient, so profitable trading strategies have limited lifespans. We can dynamically develop new ideas by deeply understanding market microstructure—how different securities markets work and how major players like hedge funds operate within various rules and structures. The goal is to find gaps where temporary opportunities arise due to constraints, costs, or informational disadvantages facing certain institutions. ChatGPT can provide advantages in comprehending market mechanics by explaining complex filings and exchange rules to reveal participation limits.

"Liquidity" refers to quickly trading an asset without substantially affecting its price. Illiquid assets have greater price frictions, making trading large amounts expensive as orders drain. Institutions avoid illiquid securities since entering big trades adversely impacts valuation. However, investing small amounts in niche illiquid assets can reveal longer valuation gaps without sophisticated arbitrage.

Informational asymmetries mean certain investors possess better predictive data or models. ChatGPT can help create and interpret alternative datasets like shipping logs or satellite imagery that would otherwise require extensive programming. By detecting early demand signals, traders can gain advantages by valuing assets and controlling risks.

Many institutional investors have strict trading rules limiting asset eligibility, which fragment markets, with complex assets attracting less smart money and enabling pricing quirks and informational edges to persist. Focused traders leveraging advanced data can exploit temporary valuation gaps in opaque niche areas neglected by status quo players concentrated on only the most liquid markets.

Implementing a profitable ChatGPT trading strategy requires continuous learning and adaptation. The core elements include understanding AI capabilities in sentiment analysis to identify signals, rigorous backtesting and risk optimization, automated execution with resilient risk management, and constant vigilance to monitor and dynamically adjust the strategy. Traders can harness AI by embracing overlooked market segments neglected by status quo players.

ChatGPT in Action: Practical Applications

This chapter explored ChatGPT's diverse financial forecasting and trading applications, from enhancing investment strategies via sentiment analysis to optimizing automated trading systems through improved order timing and risk controls. Specifically, we understood how incorporating ChatGPT can provide additional insights into market perceptions to augment traditional and quantitative investing approaches. However, while ChatGPT introduces new possibilities, we learned it is necessary to balance automation with human oversight to ensure system resilience, check overreliance on AI, and mitigate risks tied to potential model inaccuracy or lack of adaptability.

Practical Lessons

Integrating ChatGPT's sentiment analysis capabilities can significantly enhance investment strategies by providing additional insights into market perceptions beyond financial statements. Specifically, combining ChatGPT's real-time assessment of market mood with traditional indicators can create a more holistic perspective to inform stock selection and portfolio management.

Additionally, ChatGPT powerfully augments risk management practices through the early detection of negative sentiment shifts. By continuously tracking news, social media, and other data sources, ChatGPT can act as an early warning system for nascent risks. This monitoring enables preemptive actions to safeguard investments ahead of downturns.

The Future of AI in Financial Forecasting

This chapter explored the future of AI in financial forecasting, including deep learning, reinforcement learning, and the fusion of AI with blockchain and IoT. These advancements promise greater accuracy, efficiency, and breadth in financial decision-making, positioning AI as an indispensable finance tool.

However, deploying AI poses ethical and regulatory challenges around data privacy, algorithmic transparency, preventing biases, and maintaining market stability. Initiatives around data encryption, model interpretability, identifying bias, and oversight for systemic risks could enable AI's safe, fair, and effective integration. The influence of AI on finance will be transformative, reshaping jobs and firms. More intuitive, interactive interfaces will enable mass adoption. This could democratize access to sophisticated tools while challenging traditional institutions with rising demand for talent skilled in emerging technologies.

Practical Lessons

Intuitive interfaces will drive mass AI adoption. As tools leverage more automation and complexity, simplicity and customizability in user experiences become decisive for engagement. Finance should emphasize natural language processing, voice control, chatbots, and personalization to make AI accessible for professionals and investors. Usability will impact trust and utilization.

Implications

The emergence of AI poses the risk of significant disruption. Routine tasks may be automated, challenging established institutions through the rise of innovative startups. While AI democratizes sophisticated tools, it could also marginalize those lacking digital literacy.

Reskilling workforces, upgrading control mechanisms, targeting education, and measuring innovation adoption may help.

We have covered the insights and practical knowledge gained throughout our AI in finance learning journey. From grasping core concepts around markets, AI foundations, and advanced natural language models to conducting original research and developing implementable ChatGPT-driven trading strategies, this book has equipped us with capabilities to navigate the AI transformation reshaping finance. Now, we can explore what may be next for AI in finance.

The Prospects of AI in Finance

As we look toward the upcoming trends, AI will play an increasingly central role in investment methods. We will explore potential developments in AI that are set to shape the future of finance. We will cover some predictions for AI's role in future financial forecasting and how we can prepare for an AI-enhanced financial landscape.

One trend that promises to revolutionize the sector is the development of more sophisticated machine-learning algorithms. These advancements, including complex neural networks and reinforcement learning models, are set to significantly enhance AI's predictive accuracy. As these models become more refined, they can adapt better to changing market conditions, providing more precise and dynamic insights for financial applications.

Quantum computing is another intriguing development. This technology is expected to transform how complex financial models are processed. Quantum computing could dramatically reduce the time required for risk analysis, portfolio optimization, and algorithmic trading, enabling real-time decision-making and opening new paths in investment.

The integration of various AI models can also become a promising technology. By combining different AI approaches, such as deep learning combined with LLMs, and adding traditional financial models, the industry can leverage the unique strengths of each method. This hybrid approach could allow for deeper insights derived from vast datasets while maintaining the reliability of conventional finance models and tested theories.

The demand for transparent and understandable AI decisions will increase as AI integrates into finance. Explainable AI (XAI) is emerging as a solution to make AI decision-making processes more understandable to users. Understanding and trusting AI's rationale is paramount in sensitive financial contexts where decisions have significant implications. XAI provides the transparency needed to build this trust and facilitate broader AI acceptance and ethical use.

AI is expected to bring unprecedented personalization to financial services. These AI systems could offer tailored investment recommendations leveraging data on personal financial objectives, risk preferences, and market conditions. Customized investment advice, individualized risk assessments, and tailored financial planning are ways AI will cater to each client's unique needs and preferences, enhancing satisfaction and effectiveness.

Similarly, AI tools will democratize access to complex financial forecasting, leveling the playing field for smaller investors and allowing them to participate alongside larger institutions. By harnessing AI-driven insights and analyses, these investors will have the opportunity to engage in areas previously beyond their reach. This personalization of financial advice can democratize access to sophisticated investment strategies previously available only to clients with high net worth or institutional investors. As AI matures, it will further refine the personalization and effectiveness of financial advisory services, making advanced investment insights accessible to a broader range of individuals.

Developing resilient AI models that can adapt to the inherent unpredictability of financial markets will provide a lasting competitive advantage—for example, creating models that can rapidly adjust to sudden market shifts and continuously learn from new data and emerging patterns. Regular scenario analysis and stress testing of AI models against various market conditions, particularly extreme scenarios, can further enhance their resilience and reliability.

AI's application in monitoring compliance and detecting fraudulent activities is expected to expand. AI's ability to analyze transactions and behaviors at scale allows for identifying anomalies that could signify fraud or non-compliance. As regulatory demands and the complexity of financial crimes grow, AI's role in ensuring compliance and security is becoming increasingly important, marking a significant shift toward more proactive and sophisticated monitoring and enforcement in the financial industry.

Professionals in the financial sector will need to learn evolving technologies and methodologies. Simultaneously, financial institutions must invest significantly in AI skills and infrastructure, preparing their workforce to use these new tools effectively and embracing a culture of collaboration and innovation. This collaboration means fostering partnerships with tech firms, engaging in industry forums, and promoting a culture of innovation within organizations. Finally, strategic planning for AI adoption in finance must be comprehensive, considering the broader implications for business models, customer relationships, and the market.

The future of AI in finance is one of both exciting opportunities and significant challenges. By staying informed about emerging trends, preparing strategically for AI integration, and prioritizing ethical and responsible use, stakeholders in the financial sector can look forward to a future where AI not only enhances financial operations but also drives innovative and inclusive financial services.

GUIDANCE FOR STAYING AHEAD

AI rapidly transforms finance, and staying ahead means continuously learning about new technologies. This section will give you tips on keeping pace with AI advancements:

- ◆ Social Media and Local Events
  - Platforms like X (formerly Twitter) are an excellent source for the latest AI research. Follow top researchers through their social media and Google Scholar profiles.
  - Join AI groups on LinkedIn and Facebook to participate in discussions with other professionals and stay in the loop on developments.
  - Attend local AI meetups and events in your area to connect directly with peers and experts.
- ◆ Academic Research
  - The latest research is constantly published in academic journals, industry reports, technology news platforms, and conference proceedings:
  - Some top finance journals: *Journal of Finance, Review of Financial Studies, Journal of Financial Economics.*
  - Some top economic journals: *American Economic Review, Econometrica, Journal of Political Economy, Quarterly Journal of Economics, Review of Economic Studies.*

- Some leading AI conferences: NeurIPS, ICML.
- Preprint servers like arXiv and SSRN host the latest research before it gets published in academic journals.
- ◆ Hands-On Learning
  - Experiment with open-sourced code/tools like TensorFlow, PyTorch, Kaggle datasets, and notebooks.
  - Contribute to machine learning competitions on platforms like Kaggle.
- ◆ Courses and Certificates
  - Traditional courses or training programs on AI, data science, and finance from universities and online platforms.
  - Flexible online learning platforms like Coursera, EdX, and Udacity offer affordable courses from top institutions.
- ◆ Personal Development
  - Make a learning plan and dedicate time each week or month for upskilling.
  - Experiment with new techniques on personal projects and build an AI portfolio.

Moreover, we also provide recommendations on fostering innovation in a professional environment:

- ◆ Encouraging experimentation and adopting new technologies can drive growth and keep businesses at the forefront. Nurturing an environment that welcomes innovation can provide a competitive advantage.
- ◆ Allocating resources to understand the latest AI technologies and hiring talent with AI/data science expertise helps to remain competitive.
- ◆ Partnerships with tech companies, startups, and academic institutions can provide access to cutting-edge AI tools and insights through collaborative projects. Academics are usually eager to collaborate with industry.
- ◆ Robust risk management strategies are essential to assess the potential impacts of new AI tools on operations and compliance.
- ◆ Developing agile business processes that quickly adapt to new technologies is key and involves being open to changing traditional models and practices to incorporate AI-driven methods.

Staying ahead demands a multi-pronged strategy that includes ongoing education, participation in the AI community, strategic responsiveness to technological changes, and cultivating an innovative culture. By following these guidelines, you can stay up to date with the rapid progress in AI and use these technologies to gain a competitive advantage in the financial industry.

Having reviewed some strategies to remain informed, we now proceed to some of the ethical challenges that AI imposes.

THE IMPORTANCE OF ETHICAL AI

At the core of ethical AI is the commitment to responsible data use, which involves rigorous measures to ensure data privacy, secure consent for its use, and protect sensitive information. In the finance sector, handling sensitive data is a regular occurrence, and the implications of mishandling it can be severe.

Furthermore, ethical AI needs models that are fair and non-discriminatory. In finance, this means creating algorithms without biases to avoid discriminatory outcomes, such as unfair lending practices or biased investment advice.

Regular monitoring and testing of AI models continually help identify and mitigate biases. As new data is introduced and market conditions change, previously unidentified biases may surface, or new ones may develop. This ongoing process of vigilance and improvement can maintain the reliability and fairness of AI in financial applications, helping to ensure that it serves as a beneficial tool for all users.

Companies employing AI technologies must establish clear lines of accountability and mechanisms to explain and justify decisions made by AI, especially in scenarios with significant financial implications. This transparency will help maintain trust and confidence among users and stakeholders, ensuring that AI is used as a tool for enhancement rather than detriment.

Lastly, considering the broader societal impact of AI is integral. This perspective includes vigilance to ensure AI applications do not widen economic disparities and striving to make AI accessible and beneficial to a diverse range of users. Ethical AI practice involves constantly evaluating how these technologies affect society and a commitment to steering these effects toward positive and equitable outcomes.

As AI continues to permeate society, adhering to these ethical principles becomes increasingly important in shaping a future where AI contributes positively and equitably to societal progress.

FINAL THOUGHTS

As we conclude *The Predictive Edge*, it is time to reflect on our journey. This final section is dedicated to encapsulating the transformative potential of AI in finance and offering an inspirational perspective on the future of financial decision-making. It is a moment to pause and consider the implications of what we have learned and the exciting possibilities that lie ahead.

The Transformative Potential of AI in Finance

AI has marked the start of a new era in finance, marked by data-driven insights and a significant enhancement in analytical capabilities. AI's ability to process vast datasets, identify complex patterns, and generate predictive insights has revolutionized the approach to financial analysis. This shift is not just about incremental efficiency improvements; it represents a fundamental change in the understanding and interaction with financial markets. As AI continues to evolve, it's expected to deepen further and refine the analytical processes, making the financial industry more robust, responsive, and intelligent.

The transformative impact of AI is particularly evident in its empowerment of decision-makers across the financial spectrum. Financial professionals, including traders and analysts, are now equipped with AI-driven tools offering more profound, nuanced insights into the market. This empowerment extends beyond the professional sphere, reaching individual investors and effectively democratizing access to sophisticated financial analysis and decision-making tools. The broadening access to AI in finance is leveling the playing field, allowing a more comprehensive range of participants to make more informed and strategic financial decisions.

Beyond analytical enhancements, AI's transformative potential in finance significantly extends to risk management and regulatory compliance. AI is instrumental in fostering a more secure and resilient financial environment by delivering more precise risk assessments and proactively detecting anomalies and patterns indicative of fraudulent activities. Its advanced predictive capabilities and real-time analysis contribute to a more stable and trustworthy financial system, benefiting all stakeholders, from individual investors to large institutions, and ensuring the sector remains robust against existing and emerging risks.

AI is transforming traditional financial practices and making innovative financial products and services possible. The industry is witnessing the emergence of personalized investment strategies, AI-driven financial planning tools, and automated advisory services, all tailored to meet clients' varied and specific needs. These advancements are reshaping the financial services landscape, offering more customized, efficient, and accessible solutions. As AI advances, it promises to introduce further innovations to enhance the overall value and user experience of financial products and services for individuals and institutions.

Note on the Future of Financial Decision-Making

The future of AI and financial decision-making heralds a new age of data-driven and strategic insights, shaping a financial landscape that is both inclusive and efficient, catering to the nuanced needs of its many stakeholders.

As we stand on the cliff of this change, we must remain open and agile, continually polishing our skills to thrive in this technologically advanced environment. Adaptability is not just an asset; it's also necessary for those aiming to lead in the future of finance. This evolving landscape offers an unprecedented opportunity to democratize financial services, extending sophisticated analytical tools and decision-making capabilities to a broader audience, thereby fostering a more equitable financial ecosystem.

The journey toward this future needs collaborative synergies spanning financial entities, technological innovators, regulatory bodies, and academic circles. Such partnerships are pivotal in routing the application of AI in finance toward positive outcomes.

We are responsible for guiding this technological evolution with ethical integrity and transparency, ensuring that AI serves as a force for good, enhancing decision-making for the benefit of all. We can architect an AI-empowered financial domain by embracing a collective approach imbued with optimism and anchored by shared ethical principles.

The finance horizon is expanding, enriched by AI's profound capabilities. This journey demands a commitment to innovation, inclusivity, and ethical stewardship. As we progress, let us maintain a forward-thinking mindset, ready to confront the difficulties and possibilities in creating a more insightful, inclusive, and efficient financial world. *The Predictive Edge* is dedicated to informing this journey, highlighting the immense potential and the critical responsibilities of harnessing AI in financial decision-making.

INVITATION FOR FEEDBACK AND COMMUNITY ENGAGEMENT

As we conclude *The Predictive Edge*, our journey does not end here. It is the beginning of a broader conversation and a call to action for you to participate actively in the evolving narrative of AI in finance. This final section is an open invitation for feedback and community engagement aimed at fostering a vibrant community of AI enthusiasts, financial experts, and curious learners. We encourage you to share your insights and perspectives, contributing to a rich, collaborative knowledge and innovation ecosystem.

♦ We welcome you to share your input about AI in finance. Whether you're an experienced expert, an aspiring entrepreneur, or an interested observer, your perspectives are valuable. Sharing these experiences can provide real-world context to the concepts discussed in the book and inspire others. We have channels on all major social media platforms.

♦ Participating in online communities, social media channels, and discussion forums focused on AI and finance is a great way to stay engaged. These platforms offer opportunities to discuss ideas, ask questions, and connect with like-minded individuals. Engaging in these digital communities can deepen your understanding and spark innovative ideas.

♦ Writing blog posts or contributing articles to financial or tech publications can be a powerful way to engage with the community. It not only helps in sharing knowledge but also in building a personal brand in the AI and finance space.

Moreover, we invite you to participate in local AI and finance communities where you can share insights and learn from each other.

- Joining or forming local or online interest groups can help build a community of individuals passionate about AI in finance. These groups can organize meetups, webinars, workshops, and collaborative projects, creating a space for learning and sharing.
- Collaboration on research projects or practical applications of AI in finance can lead to developments. These collaborations can be between professionals from different sectors, academia, or enthusiasts working on independent projects.
- Establishing mentorship programs or networking events can be instrumental in building a supportive community. Experienced professionals can guide newcomers, fostering a culture of learning and growth.
- Ensuring the community is diverse and inclusive is vital. A diverse community brings many perspectives, enriching discussions and leading to more innovative and comprehensive solutions.
- Finally, we encourage feedback on this book. Your thoughts, critiques, and suggestions are invaluable for future editions and for making this resource as relevant and impactful as possible.

This invitation for feedback and community engagement is a call to keep the conversation going beyond this book. It is about building a dynamic and collaborative ecosystem where ideas can flourish, innovations can be fostered, and the potential of AI in finance can be fully realized. We look forward to your participation in this dynamic field.

CHECK YOUR UNDERSTANDING QUESTIONS

AI and Finance Fundamentals:
- Describe how AI, particularly large language models like ChatGPT, has transformed traditional financial analysis and decision-making processes.
- What are the primary ethical considerations when implementing AI in financial strategies?

The Evolution of AI in Business:
- How has the evolution from basic machine learning to advanced deep learning models impacted the financial industry?
- Discuss a real-world example of AI significantly influencing a business decision or strategy.

Impact of ChatGPT on Financial Forecasting:
- In what ways has ChatGPT, as a language model, contributed to financial forecasting? Provide specific examples of its applications.
- Consider the limitations of ChatGPT in stock market prediction. What are some challenges in relying solely on AI for financial forecasting?

AI-Driven Strategies in Finance:
- How can AI-driven strategies be effectively integrated into existing financial practices? Discuss the balance between AI tools and human expertise.
- Propose a scenario where an AI-driven strategy could lead to a breakthrough in financial services.

Ethical AI Use and Regulation:
- What role do transparency and accountability play in the ethical use of AI in finance? How can these be ensured?
- Discuss the importance of regulatory frameworks in governing AI applications in finance. How do they impact innovation and safety?

Emerging Trends and Future Predictions:
- Identify and explain two emerging AI technologies that can revolutionize the financial sector in the coming years.
- How do you envision the role of AI in financial decision-making evolving over the next decade?

Challenges in AI Implementation:
- Discuss the main challenges financial institutions face in implementing AI solutions. How can these challenges be addressed?
- Reflect on the importance of data quality in AI models. What are the consequences of poor data quality, and how can it be improved?

Staying Ahead in an AI-Driven World:

♦ What strategies can financial professionals employ to stay abreast of AI advancements?

♦ What strategies can businesses employ to nurture a culture of innovation and adaptability to leverage AI technologies effectively?

Continuous Innovation and Community Engagement:

♦ What actions can individuals take to engage actively in the AI and finance community?

♦ Explain why continuous innovation is crucial in AI and finance. How can this be encouraged within an organization?

APPENDIX

Check Your Understanding Answers

Chapter 1
- ◆ Stock Market Basics:
  - Stock Market's Primary Function: The stock market facilitates buying and selling stocks, allowing companies to raise capital and investors to purchase ownership stakes. It contributes to the economy by enabling capital flow, fostering economic growth, and providing a platform for price discovery and investment.
  - Common vs. Preferred Stocks: Common stocks typically, but not always, include voting rights and dividends. Preferred stocks usually do not offer voting rights but provide a claim on assets and earnings, often paying fixed dividends.
- ◆ Financial Market Types:
  - Comparison of Market Types: The stock market deals with trading company shares, reflecting corporate performance and investor sentiment. Bond markets involve debt securities, offering lower risk and fixed-income returns. Commodities markets trade physical goods, influenced by supply-demand dynamics. Forex markets involve currency trading and are vital for international trade and investment. Derivatives markets exchange contracts like futures and options based on the value of underlying assets used for hedging or speculation.

- Derivatives Function: Derivatives are instruments that derive their value from an underlying asset. Options are instruments that give the right, but not the obligation, to buy or sell an exact quantity of a security at a fixed price within a specific period. Futures are contracts allowing one to buy or sell a commodity or other instrument at a preset price within a specified period.
- ◆ Trading Principles:
  - Role of Market Makers: Market makers facilitate trading by buying and selling stocks, providing liquidity, and ensuring smoother price movements, enabling investors to execute trades more efficiently.
  - Dividends and Investment Appeal: A dividend is a distribution of a company's earnings to shareholders. Stocks offering regular dividends can attract investors seeking steady income, often reflecting the company's financial stability.
- ◆ Stock Analysis Techniques:
  - Fundamental and Technical Analysis: Fundamental analysis quantifies a company's intrinsic value based on financials and external factors. Technical analysis studies trends from trading activity, like price movements and volumes. Fundamental analysis might involve examining a company's earnings, while technical analysis could involve using moving averages to predict future price movements.
  - Importance of Volume Analysis: In technical analysis, volume analysis helps determine a price trend's strength. High trading volumes affirm the market's commitment to a price trend, while low volumes suggest a lack of conviction or potential reversal.
- ◆ Portfolio Management:
  - Diversification involves spreading investments across various assets or sectors to reduce risk. It is based on the principle that not all markets move in the same direction, so gains in one investment can offset losses in another.
  - Asset Allocation: Distributing investments across different asset categories, like stocks, bonds, and cash. It varies based on an investor's risk tolerance and investment horizon, with risk-averse investors favoring bonds and cash, while risk-tolerant investors might prefer stocks.

♦ Trading Strategies:

- Value vs. Growth Investing: Value investing focuses on under-valued stocks with solid fundamentals, expecting them to appreciate. Growth investing targets companies with the potential for significant growth, often with higher stock prices and lower dividend yields. Value investors might look at P/E ratios, while growth investors focus on future earnings potential.

- Passive Investing: Passive investing involves holding an ETF or similar instrument replicating the market. It differs from other investment styles because you do it once and do not have to pay attention to the market until you withdraw your investment.

Chapter 2

What is artificial intelligence?

♦ AI is the field under the umbrella of computer science that strives to develop machines capable of intelligent behavior. It involves the development of algorithms that empower machines to execute tasks typically demanding human intelligence, including visual perception, speech recognition, decision-making, and language translation.

What are the two fundamental aspects of intelligence discussed in the chapter?

♦ The two fundamental aspects of intelligence discussed are "understanding and adaptability" and "application and abstract thinking." Understanding and adaptability refer to learning from and adapting to new situations and challenges. Application and abstract thinking involve applying knowledge effectively and the ability to think beyond the immediate and tangible.

According to Howard Gardner's theory, can you list and describe the types of human intelligence?

♦ Per Howard Gardner's theory concerning multiple intelligences, there are several types: Linguistic (language skills), Logical-Mathematical (logical thinking and problem-solving), Spatial (visualization and spatial judgment), Musical (musical ability and appreciation), Bodily-Kinesthetic (physical coordination and skill), Interpersonal (social understanding and interaction), Intrapersonal (self-awareness and inner understanding), and Naturalistic (understanding nature and patterns).

How do computers and AI currently measure up against human intelligence?

◆ While AI can outperform humans in specific tasks, especially those involving fast data processing and pattern recognition, it generally lacks the consciousness, emotional understanding, and moral reasoning inherent in human intelligence. AI operates within set parameters and lacks humans' general adaptability and ethical judgment.

What are the different types of machine learning, and how do they work?

◆ Supervised Learning: Training the model using labeled data, learning to predict outcomes or categorize data based on past examples.

◆ Unsupervised Learning: The model identifies patterns or structures in unlabeled data, clustering similar items or reducing data dimensions without prior examples.

◆ Reinforcement Learning: The model learns to make decisions by acting in an environment to achieve a goal, receiving feedback through rewards or penalties.

How does deep learning differ from traditional machine learning?

◆ Deep learning follows machine learning principles but creates an artificial neural network with many layers, enabling it to learn and make decisions from unstructured data. Unlike traditional machine learning, which may require more human intervention and feature selection, deep learning can automatically uncover the necessary representations for feature detection or classification from unprocessed data.

What are some ethical considerations and limitations of AI?

◆ Ethical considerations include the potential for bias in decision-making, lack of transparency in decisions, and the displacement of jobs. Limitations of AI include its reliance on data quality and quantity, lack of understanding of abstract concepts, and inability to possess consciousness or emotional intelligence.

What is the Turing Test, and what are its criticisms?
- The Turing Test measures a machine's ability to exhibit intelligent behavior indistinguishable from a human. Critics argue that it focuses only on mimicking human behavior rather than understanding or consciousness and does not account for cultural biases or the complexity of human intelligence.

What are the hierarchical levels of AI, and what distinguishes them?
- Narrow AI: Focused on specific tasks with expertise in a particular domain.
- General AI (AGI): Hypothetical AI with comprehensive understanding and cognitive abilities comparable to a human being.
- Superintelligence: An advanced form of AI surpassing the brightest human minds in every field, including creative and social intelligence.

What recent advancements have led to the rise of AI models?
- Advancements include increased computational power (especially GPUs), larger and more diverse datasets, algorithmic improvements (like deep learning techniques), and the development of frameworks and libraries that democratize AI development. These advancements have enabled more complex, efficient, and accurate AI models, driving the field forward significantly.

Chapter 3

What is Natural Language Processing (NLP)?
- Answer: B. A multidisciplinary field that helps machines understand, interpret, generate, and respond to human language.

What are some critical challenges in Natural Language Processing (NLP)?
- Answer: B. Ambiguity, context understanding, sarcasm, and sentiment detection.

What is generative AI, and how does it differ from other AI forms?
- Answer: C. AI that focuses on creating new, original content based on learned patterns.

What makes Large Language Models (LLMs) effective in NLP and generative AI?
- ◆ Answer: B. Their ability to generate human-like text and understand context, thanks to training on vast datasets.

What are "hallucinations" in the context of Large Language Models?
- ◆ Answer: B. When the model generates factually incorrect, nonsensical, or unsupported outputs.

How can biases in Large Language Models impact their outputs?
- ◆ Answer: B. Biases can lead to the reinforcement of stereotypes and unfair decision-making.

What are some techniques used in NLP?
- ◆ Answer: A. Text summarization and machine translation.

Why is understanding the balance between novelty and coherence important in generative AI?
- ◆ Answer: A. It ensures that the generated content is original but also understandable and relevant.

What role does continuous learning play in the effectiveness of LLMs?
- ◆ Answer: B. It ensures that LLMs stay updated with the latest language trends and facts.

Why is addressing the issue of bias and hallucinations crucial in Large Language Models?
- ◆ Answer: B. It is crucial for maintaining AI systems' accuracy, reliability, and ethical responsibility.

Chapter 4

Self-Attention Mechanism:
- ◆ Self-Attention allows each part of the input sequence to consider and weigh other parts, enabling the model to capture context and dependencies between words or sub-parts of the input. It helps in understanding the semantics of the sentence and generating coherent and contextually appropriate text.

Transformers and Their Variations:
- ◆ Encoder-Only Model: Processes input to generate a new representation of the same, typically used in tasks like sentence classification.

- Decoder-Only Model: Generates output one piece at a time, used in generative tasks like text completion or story writing.
- Encoder-Decoder Model: The encoder processes the input, and the decoder generates the output using the encoder's representation, which is used in tasks like machine translation.

Transfer Learning:
- Transfer learning takes a pre-trained model (on a large dataset) and adapts it to a new but related problem. It's crucial in LLMs to save computational resources, improve performance, and accelerate development by leveraging previously learned patterns and knowledge.

Fine-Tuning LLMs:
- Fine-tuning involves adjusting a pre-trained model on a smaller, specific dataset, allowing it to refine its abilities and knowledge for particular tasks. Making the model more accurate and efficient for specific applications is necessary.

Adjusting Specifications:
- Model Size: Influences the model's capacity to learn complex patterns. Larger models usually perform better but require more computational resources.
- Tokenization: Affects how the text is broken down into manageable pieces, which impacts the model's understanding of the text.
- Temperature: Controls the randomness in the generation process. A higher temperature produces more creative outputs, while a lower temperature makes the outputs more predictable and conservative.
- Top-k and Top-p: These parameters control the diversity and predictability of the generated text by limiting the possible subsequent tokens to the most likely ones.

Model Comparisons:
- Answers will vary depending on the models chosen. Typically, you'd compare the number of parameters, languages supported, training data, typical applications, and unique features or capabilities.

Challenges of LLMs: The main challenges include:

◆ Computational: High resource and energy demands for training and deploying LLMs.

◆ Ethical: Risk of perpetuating biases in training data, misuse concerns, and impact on job markets.

◆ Bias-Related: Models might generate biased or harmful content reflecting biases in the training data.

Future of LLMs:

◆ Future directions include more efficient training methods, broader language support, improved understanding and generation capabilities, ethical and transparent design considerations, and novel applications in various fields.

Chapter 5

◆ ChatGPT's Training and Data Sources: ChatGPT's language capabilities are shaped by diverse and extensive data sources, enabling nuanced understanding and generation. Training with varied data enhances its adaptability across contexts.

◆ Applications in Various Sectors: ChatGPT excels in customer service, content creation, and education, automating interactions and generating tailored content.

◆ Ethical Implications of ChatGPT: Ethical concerns include privacy, bias, and misinformation. Mitigation involves transparent data handling, bias checks, and user education.

◆ Limitations of ChatGPT: Key limitations are context understanding and misinformation susceptibility, affecting reliability in complex or sensitive topics.

◆ Integration of ChatGPT in Business Operations: Businesses can integrate ChatGPT for customer support, data analysis, and automation, benefiting efficiency but facing challenges like integration complexity.

◆ Future Developments in ChatGPT and AI: Anticipated advancements may include improved contextual understanding and ethical AI practices, enhancing ChatGPT's functionality and societal impact.

♦ Regulatory and Compliance Issues: Key issues involve data privacy, ethical AI use, and sector-specific regulations, requiring careful adherence to legal and ethical standards.

♦ Continuous Learning and Adaptation in AI: Continuous learning is vital to adapt to evolving AI landscapes, necessitating ongoing education and staying informed about new developments.

Chapter 6

♦ Basic Understanding:
  • What is a long-short strategy in stock trading?
    • Answer: A long-short strategy involves buying (going long) stocks that are expected to increase in value and selling (going short) stocks that are expected to decrease in value. The goal is for the long positions to outperform the shorts, providing an overall net gain regardless of broader market direction.
  • How do ChatGPT scores of news headlines potentially predict stock price movements?
    • Answer: ChatGPT scores of news headlines evaluate the sentiment or potential market impact of the news. Stocks with positive scores might experience positive price movements, while stocks with negative scores might experience adverse price movements.

♦ In-Depth Analysis:
  • How does the complexity of news headlines, based on their readability, affect the performance of different LLMs in predicting stock returns?
    • Answer: More advanced models like GPT-3.5 and GPT-4 can interpret complex headlines, showing similar or even slightly better performance on high-complexity news than on low-complexity news. Basic models struggle with high-complexity news but may show some capability with low-complexity news.
  • How might transaction costs impact the cumulative returns of long-short strategies based on ChatGPT scores?
    • Answer: Transaction costs can reduce the returns of trading strategies. The more frequently a strategy trades, the

more it incurs these costs. In the provided example, even when considering transaction costs of up to 25 basis points (bps) per trade, the strategy based on ChatGPT scores still showed notable cumulative returns, although higher transaction costs significantly eroded returns.

♦ Future Implications:
- How could advanced LLMs reshape the financial newsrooms of the future?
  - Answer: Advanced LLMs can offer real-time sentiment analysis, predict stock price movements based on vast data, and even draft news articles or reports. This capability could lead to faster, more informed decision-making in financial newsrooms.
- Describe potential applications of language models in crisis management within the financial sector.
  - Answer: Language models could assist in analyzing vast amounts of data during a crisis to provide insights, draft communication to stakeholders, predict public reactions to statements or actions, and monitor global sentiments in real time.
- How might the integration of language models influence client interactions in wealth management?
  - Answer: Language models could enhance personalized client interactions by analyzing clients' communication to better understand their needs and concerns, drafting personalized financial plans, or providing real-time market updates tailored to individual portfolios.

♦ Critical Thinking:
- What might be some potential risks or unintended consequences of relying heavily on AI and LLMs in finance?
  - Answer: Over-reliance can lead to systemic risks if many firms use similar models, leading to correlated trading behaviors. LLMs might also misinterpret or overreact to specific information. Ethical concerns can arise if AI makes decisions humans can't understand or justify.
- How can emerging markets benefit from the sophistication brought about by advanced LLMs?

- Answer: Emerging markets can benefit from accurate sentiment analysis, better prediction of market movements, improved financial reporting and analytics, and enhanced investor communications, potentially leading to increased foreign investments and financial stability.
- ◆ Application:
  - Imagine you're a financial analyst at a hedge fund. How might you incorporate insights from LLMs like ChatGPT into your daily decision-making process?
    - Answer: Insights from ChatGPT can be used to gauge market sentiment, analyze news headlines for potential stock impacts, and even draft or refine reports. ChatGPT can assist in sifting through large volumes of news and data to highlight potentially important market-moving information.
  - What would it look like if you were to design a new financial product leveraging the capabilities of advanced LLMs? Discuss its potential benefits and challenges.
    - Answer: One could design an AI-driven investment fund where LLMs constantly analyze global news, market data, and investor sentiments to make real-time investment decisions. Benefits include rapidly processing vast amounts of information and potentially uncovering hidden market opportunities. Challenges include over-reliance on technology, potential misinterpretations by the AI, and the need for constant oversight and refinement of the model.

Chapter 7

- ◆ Sentiment Analysis and Trading Signals: ChatGPT uses sentiment analysis to identify trading signals by analyzing news articles for positive or negative sentiment toward companies. It looks for keywords, phrases, and contextual cues that indicate favorable or unfavorable sentiment, such as "record profits" or "management issues." Optimistic sentiment might lead to a positive position signal. In contrast, negative sentiment could trigger a short position signal.

◆ Position Sizing in the Portfolio: Limiting each position to no more than 2% of the portfolio is crucial for risk diversification and management. This rule ensures that the portfolio doesn't have excessive exposure to the performance of a single stock, thereby reducing the impact of individual stock volatility and promoting a balanced investment approach.

◆ Mean-Variance Optimization: The strategy employs mean-variance optimization with inverse stock variance weighting to balance the portfolio for risk and return. This approach involves assigning higher weights to stocks with lower variance (less volatility) and lower weights to those with higher variance. This method helps stabilize the portfolio, aiming to reduce the impact of volatile stocks on overall performance.

◆ Backtesting the Strategy: Backtesting is significant, as it evaluates how the strategy would have performed under past market conditions. It assists in pinpointing the strategy's strengths and weaknesses. However, pitfalls like overfitting historical data and assuming future market behavior will mirror the past should be carefully considered and avoided.

◆ Automating Trade Execution: Automating trade execution ensures timely and disciplined execution of trades based on the strategy's criteria. It helps in maintaining consistency and reacting quickly to sentiment changes. Challenges include ensuring the accuracy of automated systems and the need for periodic reviews to adjust for market changes.

◆ Risk Management Practices: Key risk management practices include setting stop-loss orders, diversifying across sectors, and continuously monitoring portfolio risk metrics like volatility and correlation. These practices help mitigate risks associated with individual stock performance and broader market fluctuations.

◆ Adapting to Market Changes: Ongoing monitoring and adjustments are necessary due to the ever-changing nature of financial markets and the possibility of swift shifts in news sentiment. Adjustments may be required in response to market volatility, significant news events affecting specific stocks or sectors, or changes in overall market sentiment.

◆ Ethical Considerations and Compliance: Ethical considerations include ensuring transparency in AI decision-making processes and avoiding market manipulation. Adhering to regulatory requirements helps prevent legal issues and maintain market integrity. These aspects help ensure the responsible use of AI in trading and to strengthen investor trust.

◆ Continuous Learning in AI-Driven Trading: Continuous learning and adaptation are important due to the rapidly evolving nature of AI technology and financial markets. Traders can stay informed through ongoing education, engaging with professional communities, and staying updated with the latest AI developments and regulatory changes in the financial sector.

Chapter 8

◆ How does ChatGPT enhance traditional investment strategies with its sentiment analysis capabilities?

   ● ChatGPT enhances traditional investment strategies by providing real-time, nuanced sentiment analysis, offering investors insights into market mood and perceptions that might not be immediately evident in financial statements or macroeconomic data.

◆ Describe how risk management benefits from integrating ChatGPT's predictive capabilities.

   ● Risk management benefits from integrating ChatGPT's predictive capabilities by using its early warning system to detect potential negative shifts in market sentiment, allowing investors to take preemptive actions to safeguard investments and minimize potential losses.

◆ Explain the role of ChatGPT in automated trading systems and how it affects decision-making.

   ● In automated trading systems, ChatGPT contributes by analyzing market sentiment and translating it into quantitative signals. This integration helps make more informed and timely trading decisions, increasing the systems' profitability and risk-adjusted returns.

- ◆ What steps are involved in combining sentiment analysis with a quantitative momentum strategy?
  - The steps involved in combining sentiment analysis with a quantitative momentum strategy include collecting and analyzing real-time data for high-momentum stocks, integrating sentiment scores from ChatGPT with momentum signals, and using the combined model to refine investment decisions and mitigate risks.
- ◆ Identify the challenges and limitations of relying solely on AI for investment risk management.
  - The challenges and limitations of AI for risk management include the potential for false positives, the inability to capture highly nuanced human insights, and the need for a balanced approach that combines human expertise and traditional methods.
- ◆ Detail how real-time sentiment analysis by ChatGPT can lead to proactive risk mitigation.
  - Real-time sentiment analysis by ChatGPT leads to proactive risk management by continuously monitoring and analyzing market sentiments to detect early signs of negative shifts, enabling investors to adjust their strategies before substantial financial impacts occur.
- ◆ Discuss the importance of balancing AI insights with traditional investment risk assessment methods.
  - Balancing AI insights with traditional investment risk assessment methods is essential to create a more holistic and robust strategy. While AI provides valuable predictive and real-time analysis, traditional methods ensure a comprehensive understanding of financial health, market position, and macroeconomic conditions.

Chapter 9

- ◆ Advancements in AI Technologies: Emerging AI technologies impacting financial forecasting include deep learning, reinforcement learning, and bespoke neural networks for finance. These advancements differ from traditional methods by offering enhanced pattern recognition, predictive modeling, and real-time adaptation to market conditions.

◆ Integration of AI with Blockchain and IoT: AI can enhance the reliability and integrity of financial data. At the same time, AI combined with IoT can provide diverse real-time data sources. Applications include secure, transparent transaction recording and holistic market analysis using real-time IoT data.

◆ Data Processing and Personalization in AI: AI contributes to efficiency in data analysis through its ability to rapidly process large volumes of complex data and identify market trends. Personalization in AI offers tailored financial advice and strategies based on individual investor profiles, leading to more effective investment outcomes.

◆ Navigating the Regulatory Landscape: Key regulatory challenges include ensuring transparency, preventing algorithmic bias, and maintaining data privacy. Addressing these challenges is crucial for AI's credibility and ethical implementation in financial decision-making.

◆ Ethical Considerations and Data Privacy: Potential AI model biases and data misuse concerns are primary ethical dilemmas. Addressing these concerns involves implementing stringent data privacy measures, ensuring model transparency, and regular auditing for discrimination.

◆ Overcoming AI Limitations: Current limitations include data-quality issues, model opacity, and algorithmic bias. Future developments, like improved data processing and more transparent models, can address these. Adaptable AI models are crucial for responding to market volatility.

◆ AI's Influence on the Financial Industry: AI will likely automate routine tasks, leading to job displacement in some areas but creating new roles in AI and data science. It could challenge traditional financial institutions and lead to new entities like AI-driven investment funds and robo-advisors.

◆ Investor Education and AI Literacy: Education and literacy are crucial for understanding AI tools and strategies, assessing AI-driven investment opportunities, and making informed decisions. Enhanced AI literacy can lead to better investment outcomes and more widespread adoption of AI in finance.

◆ Development of Interactive AI Interfaces: Future advancements may include more intuitive designs, natural language processing features for user interaction, customization options, and seamless integration with other financial tools. These will enhance user engagement and make AI insights more accessible.

Chapter 10

AI and Finance Fundamentals:

♦ AI, especially large language models like ChatGPT, has revolutionized financial analysis by enabling unprecedented forecasting power using unstructured data like news and social media for sentiment analysis and market trend predictions. The primary ethical considerations include ensuring data privacy, avoiding biased decision-making, maintaining transparency, and adhering to regulatory standards.

The Evolution of AI in Business:

♦ The shift from basic machine learning to advanced deep learning has enabled more nuanced and sophisticated analyses of financial data, leading to more accurate predictions and personalized financial services. An example is the use of AI in risk assessment, where AI algorithms can analyze large datasets to identify potential risks more efficiently than traditional methods.

Impact of ChatGPT on Financial Forecasting:

♦ ChatGPT has contributed to financial forecasting by analyzing news and financial reports for sentiment analysis, helping predict stock market trends. However, its limitations include potential biases in training data and the inability to fully understand or predict market dynamics influenced by unpredictable external factors.

AI-Driven Strategies in Finance:

♦ AI-driven strategies can be integrated into financial practices by complementing human expertise with AI's data processing capabilities, ensuring a balanced approach that leverages both strengths. A hypothetical scenario could involve using AI for real-time market sentiment analysis to inform trading strategies in a hedge fund, leading to improved returns.

Ethical AI Use and Regulation:

◆ Transparency and accountability are crucial in ethical AI use to ensure that AI-driven decisions can be understood and justified, particularly in high-stakes financial contexts. Regulatory frameworks are essential for balancing safety and innovation, setting standards for responsible AI use while encouraging technological advancement.

Emerging Trends and Future Predictions:

◆ Two emerging technologies with transformative potential are quantum computing, which can process complex financial models at unprecedented speeds, and hybrid AI models that combine different AI approaches for more robust financial analysis. In the next decade, AI will likely become more integrated into decision-making processes, with advancements in AI leading to more sophisticated and personalized financial services.

Challenges in AI Implementation:

◆ The main challenges include ensuring data quality, aligning AI strategies with business goals, and addressing ethical concerns and regulatory compliance. Addressing these challenges involves investing in data management, aligning AI use with a clear strategic vision, and establishing ethical guidelines and compliance checks.

Staying Ahead in an AI-Driven World:

◆ Financial professionals can stay ahead by continuously learning through courses, webinars, and conferences, being informed about industry developments, and participating in professional networks. Businesses can establish a culture that encourages experimentation, invests in employee AI training, and adapts to new technologies to foster innovation.

Continuous Innovation and Community Engagement:

◆ Individuals can engage in the AI and finance community by participating in forums, attending conferences, contributing to research, and collaborating on projects. Continuous innovation is essential to keep pace with rapid technological changes and can be encouraged by fostering an environment that values creativity, supports risk-taking, and promotes lifelong learning.

References

Anthropic. 2023. "Introducing Claude." Anthropic. https://www .anthropic.com/index/introducing-claude.

Awadallah, Ahmed. 2023. "Orca 2: Teaching Small Language Models How to Reason." Microsoft. https://www.microsoft.com/en-us/ research/blog/orca-2-teaching-small-language-models-how-to-reason/.

BigScience. 2023. "Introducing The World's Largest Open Multilingual Language Model: BLOOM." BigScience. Accessed December 31, 2023. https://bigscience.huggingface.co/blog/bloom.

Binet, Alfred, Theophile Simon, and Elizabeth S. Kite. 2017. The Development of Intelligence in Children (the Binet-Simon Scale). N.p.: Trieste Publishing Pty Limited.

Cherry, Kendra. 2023. "Gardner's Theory of Multiple Intelligences." Verywell Mind. March 11, 2023. https://www.verywellmind.com/ gardners-theory-of-multiple-intelligences-2795161.

Cohere. n.d. Cohere | The leading AI platform for enterprise. Accessed December 26, 2023. https://cohere.com/.

Cohere Team. 2022. "LLM Parameters Demystified: Getting the Best Outputs from Language AI." https://txt.cohere.com/llm-parameters-best-outputs-language-ai/.

Collins, Elli. 2021. "LaMDA: Our breakthrough conversation technology." https://blog.google/technology/ai/lamda/.

Devlin, Jacob, and Ming Chang. 2018. "Open Sourcing BERT: State-of-the-Art Pre-training for Natural Language Processing." Google Research Blog. https://blog.research.google/2018/11/open-sourcing-bert-state-of-art-pre.html.

Gardner, Howard. 1993. Frames of mind: The theory of multiple intelligences. N.p.: Basic Books.

Google. n.d. "Google AI PaLM 2 – Google AI." Google AI. Accessed December 31, 2023. https://ai.google/discover/palm2.

Google Deepmind. n.d. "Gemini." Google DeepMind. Accessed December 31, 2023. https://deepmind.google/technologies/gemini/#introduction.

Ivankov, Alex. 2023. "LLaMA Explained: Capabilities and Differentiation." Profolus. https://www.profolus.com/topics/llama-explained-capabilities-and-differentiation/.

Jones, Cameron, and Benjamin Bergen. 2023. "Does GPT-4 Pass the Turing Test?" arxiv.org. https://arxiv.org/abs/2310.20216?s=08.

LaMDA: 2021. Our breakthrough conversation technology. The Keyword. https://blog.google/technology/ai/lamda/.

Llama 2. n.d. Meta AI. Accessed December 29, 2023. https://ai.meta.com/llama/.

López, Francisco J. 2023. "Introducing the Prompt Engineering Canvas." Medium.com. https://flopezlira.medium.com/crafting-effective-ai-prompts-2f0decfb87a3.

Lopez-Lira, Alejandro, and Yuehua Tand, Can ChatGPT Forecast Stock Price Movements? Return Predictability and Large Language Models (April 6, 2023). Available at SSRN: https://ssrn.com/abstract=4412788 or http://dx.doi.org/10.2139/ssrn.4412788

McCarthy, J., M. L. Minsky, N. Rochester, and C. E. Shannon n.d. "A Proposal for the Dartmouth Summer Research Project on Artificial Intelligence" Accessed December 26, 2023. https://doi.org/10.1609/aimag.v27i4.1904.

Merriam-Webster. n.d. "Intelligence Definition & Meaning." Merriam-Webster. Accessed December 26, 2023. https://www.merriam-webster.com/dictionary/intelligence.

Microsoft. 2023. "Orca 2: Teaching Small Language Models How to Reason." Microsoft. https://www.microsoft.com/en-us/research/blog/orca-2-teaching-small-language-models-how-to-reason/.

Mukherjee, Shaoni. n.d. "Introducing Falcon 180b: A Comprehensive Guide with a Hands-On Demo of the Falcon 40B." Paperspace Blog. Accessed December 31, 2023. https://blog.paperspace.com/introducing-falcon/.

Norouzi, Armin. 2023. "Evaluating Large Language Models: Methods, Best Practices & Tools | Lakera – Protecting AI teams that disrupt the world." Lakera AI. https://www.lakera.ai/blog/large-language-model-evaluation.

Norvig, Peter. 2023. "Has Any AI Passed the Turing Test?" Artificial Intelligence +. https://www.aiplusinfo.com/blog/has-any-ai-passed-the-turing-test/.

Roberts, Jacob. 2016. "Thinking Machines: The Search for Artificial Intelligence." Science History Institute. https://www.sciencehistory.org/stories/magazine/thinking-machines-the-search-for-artificial-intelligence/.

Rosenblatt, Frank. 1957. "The perceptron: A perceiving and recognizing automaton (project para)." https://bpb-us-e2.wpmucdn.com/websites.umass.edu/dist/a/27637/files/2016/03/rosenblatt-1957.pdf.

Turing, Alan M. 1950. "COMPUTING MACHINERY AND INTELLIGENCE." MIND LIX, no. 236 (October). https://academic.oup.com/mind/article/LIX/236/433/986238.

UC Today. 2023. "The Best Large Language Models in 2023: Top LLMs." UC Today. https://www.uctoday.com/unified-communications/the-best-large-language-models-in-2023-top-llms/.

Warrington, Stuart D. 2023. "The 'What,' 'Why' and 'How' of Needs Assessment for Adult ESL Learners." https://core.ac.uk/download/72791264.pdf.

Waters, Richard. 2023. "Man beats machine at Go in human victory over AI." Ars Technica. https://arstechnica.com/information-technology/2023/02/man-beats-machine-at-go-in-human-victory-over-ai/.

Werbos, Paul J. 1990. "Backpropagation through time: What it does and how to do it - Proceedings of the IEEE." Neural Network and Machine Learning Laboratory. https://axon.cs.byu.edu/Dan/678/papers/Recurrent/Werbos.pdf.

Acknowledgments

I am deeply grateful for the support of my father, Francisco Lopez-Lira, for his invaluable input in making this draft. I am also thankful to my coauthor, Yuehua Tang, for his outstanding work in our research.

About the Author

Alejandro Lopez-Lira's research centers on machine learning, asset pricing, stock return predictability, and large language models—the core topics of this book. He holds a Finance PhD from Wharton and an economics degree from ITAM. Dr. Lopez-Lira has practical experience advising hedge funds on implementing AI strategies over the past years.

His recent awards include the 2023 BlackRock Best Paper Prize for the research underpinning this book. Other recent awards and grants include the Australian Stock Exchange Prize for Best Paper in Derivatives, the Best Paper Award for Financial Stability 2023, the Jacobs Levy Center Research Paper Prize for Outstanding Paper in 2022, the Best Paper Award: Invesco IQS Factor Investing Prize in 2021, and the Jacobs Levy Equity Management Center for Quantitative Financial Research Grant in 2020.

Index